Contemporary Basketry

CONTEM-PORARY BASKET-RY

Sharon Robinson

Davis Publications, Inc.

Worcester, Massachusetts

Printed in the United States of America
Library of Congress Catalog Card Number: 77-92139
ISBN 0-87192-097-2

Composition: Davis Press, Inc.
Printing and Binding: Halliday Lithograph
Type: Melior
Graphic Design: Jane Pitts

Consulting Editors: George F. Horn and Sarita R. Rainey

10   9   8   7   6   5   4   3   2   1

CON-
TENTS

To my daughter Cathie

I'd like to thank all the basket makers who kindly sent me or allowed me to take photos of their work. My thanks also to those who put me in contact with basket makers with whom I was not yet acquainted.

I'm also grateful to the people from whom I've taken classes or workshops in basketry: Lee DeKoker, Shereen LaPlantz, Lucy Traber, and Lydia VanGelder. And, thanks to my daughter who posed for the photos showing the basket techniques, and who helped me read the manuscript.

Contemporary Basketry

The texture on this tree could
have been the inspiration for
Holey Basket by the author.

INTRO-
DUCTION

Holey Basket by the author.

Basketry, together with many other crafts, has now become a very popular art form. Since the 1960s, it has been accepted as a fine art medium. At one time, baskets were primarily made for utilitarian purposes. Today, even though plastic, ceramic, and metal containers fulfill these needs, basketry, whether functional or not, is actively appreciated for its aesthetic value.

The precise origins of basketry are unknown, yet many feel it predates pottery. Evidence suggests that basketry developed as a result of people's needs to survive. Impressions of baskets found in clay indicate that they once functioned as molds for clay cooking vessels. People needed these vessels as well as other containers for cooking, gathering and storing materials, and for snaring prey. Basketry techniques were also used for building, clothing, and ceremonial objects. For example, broad-leafed materials were thatched for roofs and used for bedding. Remnants of hats and sandals reveal that they too were once woven according to basketry techniques.

Since baskets grew out of people's needs, their forms were both influenced and restricted by the materials that were available and by the conditions in which these materials grew. Different fibers grow in different climates. Thus, as we shall see in this study, a great variety of woven basketry items have developed.

Upon deciding to learn basketry, you will no doubt wonder how to begin, where to get ideas, and how to transform your ideas into a basket.

First, learn the basic techniques of the craft and use materials that are easiest to handle. Recommended materials are described in the beginning of each chapter. It is important not to make the task of learning techniques more difficult by using materials that are stiff and unwieldy. Once you master the suggested techniques, then experiment with them in various designs and materials.

Nature has always been an abundant source of inspiration. It not only provides excellent materials for basketry, but suggests endless ways to design them. Look around at the grasses and trees. Watch the way the gourds grow in your garden. Take a stroll on the beach; study the waves, clouds, and sand. What a wealth of interesting textures and shapes there are! Attempt to see everything around you with a new and fresh viewpoint. Translate what you see into your work.

Kelp basket of knotless netting by Carol Stinton. This basket retains the tangled feeling of the kelp.

Triangles are often used in American Indian basketry. Here the author uses the traditional Indian motif in a contemporary basket.

Materials may be another source of inspiration. Look at a pile of kelp on the beach. Study how it loops over and around itself. This is an excellent example of how materials can inspire and dictate shape. In its natural state, kelp looks like loops; therefore, the looping technique may be appropriate for construction. Kelp is slippery and can be difficult to shape during construction, hence a simple shape results.

Begin to notice the shapes of baskets and containers you see in stores, books, museums, and other places. There is no harm in using a shape someone has used before. Remember nothing is totally new; use classic shapes and give them your own interpretation. American Indian baskets have always been a source of inspiration. It is important to study the works of the American Indians as they have developed the techniques of basketry into a fine art. The design and workmanship of their baskets are superb and result in part from their use of classic design patterns and shapes.

Perhaps you will gain inspiration from an unusual old basket. Give an old idea a contemporary twist. This old Chinese tea basket, purchased at a second-hand store, inspired *Beverage Basket.*

The use for a traditional or contemporary basket or container might give you an idea. Perhaps thinking of what could be found within could be inspiring. Baskets and containers can be used for holding waste paper, flowers, water, eggs, and perhaps even snakes.

After you study basketry, you will be aware of the many items that are made from basketry techniques. Soon you will be able to experience the pleasure of identifying the construction techniques of every basket you see. You will closely inspect not only the baskets you own, but also those in stores and museums. Furthermore, you will realize that many clothing, furniture, and accessory items are made using basket techniques.

Today, the emphasis in basketry is to learn the basic techniques and then to reinterpret them so that they will conform to your experience. Feel free to alter the basic methods to suit your own ideas and needs. Examples of these methods as well as imaginative applications of them are presented in numerous photographs and illustrations. They should inspire creative, new ideas within you.

This old Chinese tea basket carries a tea pot and two cups.

Beverage Basket by author carries glassware for the beverage of your choice.

Instead of eggs in the basket, the baskets are in the egg. *Don't Put all your Baskets in One Egg* by Jessica Scarborough.

This basket was inspired by the snake baskets from India. *Snake in a Basket* by author. 8" tall, 7" in diameter. The basket was coiled with handspun wool around a jute foundation cord reinforced with wire. The snake is made of cardboard, cotton batting, and nylon stocking, with the pattern stitched on the snake after completion.

MATERI-
ALS

Selecting materials offers an exciting challenge to the basket maker. Many materials may be used for making baskets—beautiful handspun wools, "wild" plant fibers that you collect yourself, or exciting synthetics discovered in unexpected places. Your choice is limited only by the limits of your imagination. Experiment with many fibers to get the "feel" of their handling. You will soon discover which you enjoy using the most, and which are more appropriate for your design.

Before we begin our discussion of materials, an important distinction must be made. Most baskets include these two elements: the warp and the weft. The warp is the foundation cord, which forms the structure of the basket. The weft holds the structure together. Because it sometimes wraps around the warp, it can be called the wrapping material. Yarns are often used as a weft or wrapping material because they are pliable, manageable, and available in a wide variety of forms. Yarns may be synthetic or made of animal or plant fibers. Some will have soft qualities, while others will be harsh and rough. Some have a sheen and others are dull or fuzzy. Thick or thin, loosely or tightly spun—all these characteristics will contribute to your basket.

Check the yarns at your local hand weaving supplier and compare their differences.

Stiffer materials, such as some ropes, cords, and reeds, may be used for the warp or foundation cord because of their strength. The fiber content and size of these materials will vary according to your needs. Remember to check hardware stores as well as hand weaving supply shops to find these items.

You should by no means feel that the only available materials are those that you can buy. What about those "wild" plant fibers you gather yourself? Baskets made of plant fibers evoke a sense of pure and uncorrupted nature. This feeling is especially created if the materials are used in their natural state, without preparation that may make them look as if they were purchased.

An assortment of rug wool, chenille, synthetic blends, and handspuns. Courtesy of The Handweaver, Sonoma, California.

Raffia makes a good weft; reed or sea grass is a strong warp. Courtesy of The Handweaver, Sonoma, California.

Cotton and jute cords are available in many sizes and colors.

Wild basket by Lucy Traber. The basket is made of looped kelp and is 28″ in diameter. Photograph courtesy of the artist.

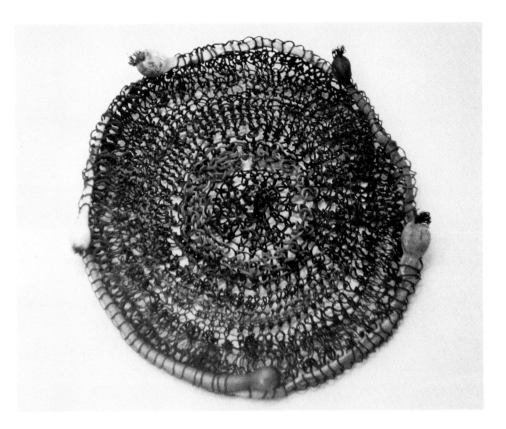

Many exciting basket materials may be found in your own backyard, or gathered on an afternoon outing. Some materials can be salvaged from the gardener at the local park or college campus on pruning days. However, if you wish to gather materials on unfamiliar lands, be sure to investigate local regulations. In many areas you may be violating the law if you pick materials.

Synthetic materials can be very exciting. Those that are capable of being woven together are suitable for basketry. Materials can be found in the kitchen, garage, or hardware store. Try wire, plastic tubing, cellophane, and nylon clothesline.

Accessories, such as feathers, beads, and shells, are often used to give a basket a finished look. An accessory may even be the inspiration for a basket.

Not many tools are required in basket making. Those that you use will be determined by the materials and techniques that you choose.

It is very important to become familiar with the inherent qualities of your materials as they will both inspire and restrict your design. You can only determine which materials will aid you in expressing an idea and which will work against you by experimenting and working with several materials. This process of discovering, of realizing the potentials and limitations of each substance, will aid you significantly in your work. For example, you may learn that a stiff foundation cord is not flexible enough to shape a basket by the coiling technique. Alternatively, you may realize that although you have chosen the right material, you do not know how to control it. When constructing a pine needle basket, for example, the pine needles may break every time you pass the needle through them. Perhaps your sewing needle is too large, the pine needles are too fine, or you did not soak them beforehand. There are always many reasons your work may not be going as planned. These problems can be overcome in time by a willingness to experiment and to explore the properties of your materials.

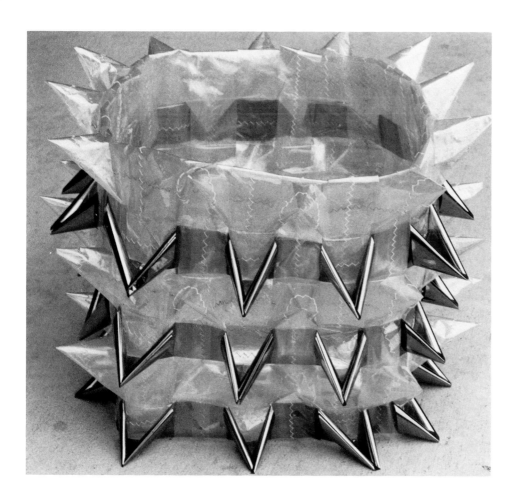

Mace, by author, was constructed from mylar and cellophane.

A strip of fur, beads, bells, and an assortment of feathers can all be used to ornament a basket.

COILING

(above)
Ikat Basket by Lydia Van Gelder. 17" tall, 10" in diameter. The wrapping material is handspun and commercial wool dyed with indigo, worked in the figure eight stitch. The foundation material is cotton cord reinforced with wire. The patterned areas have been created by ikat, a resist dye technique. Picaci shells and feathers finish the basket. Collection of Mr. and Mrs. Roger vonRosenberg.

One of the most versatile and popular basketry techniques is coiling. In coiling there are only two elements, the warp and the weft. As stated earlier, the warp is the foundation cord and the weft is the wrapping material. After you master the start of the basket (the most difficult part), the different ways of wrapping, and some of the ways of adding accessories, you can begin to use this knowledge in an imaginative way.

The following materials, which are easy to handle, are suggested for making samplers of the basic techniques:

Hands coiling.

1. Jute makes a good foundation cord. It is easy to work with since it is pliable, yet has body to hold its shape. Use three or four ply jute that is about one-quarter of an inch in diameter.

2. A yarn with body, like rug wool, is useful as wrapping material. For a sampler, do not choose a yarn, such as knitting worsted, that will stretch or yarn that is very lumpy or loosely spun, like some handspuns. It may wear as you work.

3. A tapestry needle is also required, the eye of which will fit the yarn.

4. Scissors are always needed.

After you try one basket you will want to try another, so you will want needles, yarns, and foundation cords of many sizes and types.

Dr. Seuss Basket by author. 16" tall, 7" in diameter. The foundation material is Mexican handspun which has not been completely covered with a synthetic yarn wrapping material in the figure eight stitch. The lid was covered with looped yarn, some of which was cut and tied in knots.

Trinket Basket by author. 2" tall, 3" wide, 2" deep. This coiled basket was made by wrapping raffia in the figure eight stitch over a reed foundation cord.

COILING

Sand Layers by Shannon Murray. 12" tall, 22" in diameter, 6" in circumference. The foundation cord is a large reed. The wrapping material is a combination of handspun goat and camel hair and commercial wools in beige and grey. It was constructed entirely with the figure eight stitch.

Oreo Basket by Carole Lee. 6" tall, 4" in diameter. Wool wrapping material was used over a jute foundation cord. Feathers and pattern give a whimsical look to this basket, constructed with figure eight stitches.

Janus Face Masket by Marcia Floor. 3" tall, 11" wide, 12" long. This basket is coiled with lazy squaw and knot stitches. Made of leather strips, it is reversible.

COILING

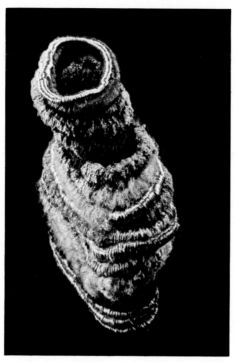

(far left)
Shield #1 by Larry Edman. 18" in diameter. A coiled basket with a wool wrapping material on a cotton foundation. The pile area on the lower half is extended with the use of glass beads and feathers. Photograph courtesy of the artist, private collection.

(left)
Jar S. P. by Cheryl Glazer. 7" tall, 5" wide, 3" deep. This jar was coiled with the figure eight stitch using rayon, wool, mohair yarns, and copper and steel wire over a welt foundation cord. Photograph courtesy of the artist.

Canoe Basket by Lydia Van Gelder. 6" wide, 12" long, 3" tall. The wrapping material is handspun wool with natural dyes, worked over a jute foundation in a figure eight stitch. Pheasant feathers finish the basket.

COILING

Afrikaans by Ellen Jones. 9″ tall, 3″ in diameter. This twined basket, using jute for the warp and weft, has a knotted bottom. Photograph courtesy of the artist.

Basket by Patricia Malarcher. 14″ tall. The blue, red, white, and yellow goat hair weft twines over a jute warp material. Photograph courtesy of the artist.

TWINING

Sun in Leo, Moon in Cancer by Marcia Floor. 10" wide, 11" long, 7" tall. Wrapped twining in leather strips forms the body of this basket with a mask of leather at the bottom. Fur outlines its opening.

Wind Gatherer by Louise Robbins. 7" tall. Twined with wool over a rope warp. Photograph courtesy of the artist.

Gourd Basket by Jan Parker. 12" tall. Twined with linen and wool, the foundation of this basket is a gourd. Photograph courtesy of the artist.

Basket of Fleece by Judy Galvin. 12" in diameter, 14" tall. This basket has been twined and wrapped, using raw fleece as a finishing material, and wool as the weft. Photograph courtesy of the artist.

Bark and Fabric Basket by Peggy Moulton. 10" tall, 8" in diameter. Remnants of a wool sweater, upholstery material, and knit fabric twine and weave around a eucalyptus bark warp.

PLAITING

Basket by Shereen LaPlantz. 18" by 18". This basket was first woven of paper fiber splint, then embellished with grosgrain and satin ribbon in the sixth Algonquin technique. The lip and handle are stitched with waxed linen. Photograph by David M. LaPlantz.

Rainbow Basket by Peggy Moulton. 14" tall. This basket has been plaited of strips of fabric of various types, such as cotton, knits, and silk. The strips were cut on the bias from pieced fabric. The strips were then slightly stuffed and hand stitched. Photograph courtesy of the artist.

PLAITING

Meander Basket by Marcia Floor. 9″ long, 6″ wide, 3″ tall. This basket was plaited with rawhide strips. Beach pebbles are tossed into the bottom of the basket and used for eyes on the snakes.

Basket by Patricia Malarcher. 6″ tall. This basket was plaited of goat hair and finished with linen wrapped ends. Photograph courtesy of the artist.

Wall Hanging by Lida Gordon. 11″ wide, 14″ tall. Flat braids of silk have been plaited to create this wall hanging. Photograph courtesy of the artist.

(far left)
Indian Tower by Earl G. Snellenberger. 38″ tall, 12½″ in diameter at the widest point. ¼″ wide strips of light and dark gold mylar plastic were plaited to create this basket. Photograph courtesy of the artist.

(left)
Golden Spire by Earl G. Snellenberger. 4½′ tall, 12″ in diameter at the widest point. Plaited with ½″ wide strips of dark gold mylar plastic. Photograph courtesy of the artist.

PLAITING

Basket by Richard C. Schneider. 20″ tall. This is a black ash splint pack basket. Also shown are some splints and a pounder for loosening the splints from the log. Photograph courtesy of the artist.

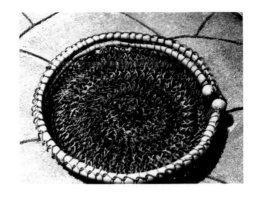

Wild Basket by Lucy Traber. 28″ in diameter, 4″ deep. This basket was looped flat to the perimeter where the large piece of kelp was looped in to form the sides of the basket. Photograph courtesy of the artist.

Basket by Ellen Hauptil. 8″ in diameter, 6″ tall. This basket has been twined of palm leaves. Notice the top edges of the palm have been folded back in to finish the piece. Photograph courtesy of the artist.

Coiled Sweetgrass Basket by Dorothy Gill Barnes. 5″ in diameter, 6″ tall. Photograph courtesy of the artist.

WILD BASKET MATERIALS

Two Pine Needle Baskets by Carole Lee. 3″ tall, 5″ in diameter, 4″ tall, 3″ in diameter. Constructed with raffia in the wheat stitch over pine needles.

Bullrush Bowl by author. 8″ in diameter, 3″ tall. Bullrush wrapped with raffia in the split stitch.

Small Pine Needle Basket by author. 4″ in diameter, 3″ tall. Courtesy of Kathleen Allen.

WILD BASKET MATERIALS

(far left)
Felt-crocheted basket by author.
8″ in diameter, 4″ tall. Crocheted
handspun white wool was felted
to grey wool on the inside.
Guinea hen feathers were attached
after completion.

(left)
Desert Sunset by Ellen Jones.
12″ by 13″. This basket was knotted
with jute and linen. Photograph by
Arthur Jones.

Six Baskets by Renie Breskin
Adams. 3½″ to 13″ tall. These bas-
kets are crocheted of mixed fibers.
Photograph courtesy of the artist.

Ikat Basket #2 by Larry Edman.
This basket has been half hitched
from a coiled base; the lid is also
coiled. The material used is silk
ikat—a resist dye technique on
linen. Photograph courtesy
of the artist.

NON TRADITIONAL BASKET TECHNIQUES

Cosmic Bowl, Inner Eye by Renie Breskin Adams. 20″ tall, 11″ wide, 3″ deep. This piece, made with cotton yarn, has been crocheted and double half hitched. Detail photograph courtesy of the artist.

(left)
Crocheted Basket by Lynn Lewbel. 9″ in diameter, 14″ tall. Many colored tapestry wool yarns were crocheted over a reed foundation cord to give a coiled appearance.

(far left)
Still Life Pillow by Renie Breskin Adams. 5″ tall, 10″ in diameter. This piece has been constructed of half hitches and crochet, using cotton yarns. Photograph courtesy of the artist.

NON TRADITIONAL BASKET TECHNIQUES

Polychrome Basket #1 by Larry Edman. This basket has been half hitched with cotton embroidery floss on a linen foundation. Photograph courtesy of the artist.

(left)
Pantyhose Basket by Peggy Moulton. 8″ diameter, 4″ tall. This machine stitched basket is made from dryer lint, assorted threads, and pantyhose.

(far left)
Hemp Rope Piece by Carolyn Thomas. 3′8″ long, 1′6″ wide. This unusually shaped basket of hemp rope is made with double half hitches. Note the two internal container compartments in the upper and lower regions. Photograph by Neil MacEwan.

Teapot Basket by Renie Breskin Adams. 4½″ tall. This basket was crocheted with cotton yarns. Photograph courtesy of the artist.

NON TRADITIONAL BASKET TECHNIQUES

(above)
Recycling Mary's Dress by Peggy Moulton. 12" tall, 8" in diameter. Cotton knit fabric has been worked in looping or knotless netting.

(above, right)
Pouch and Lid by Diane Itter. 3" in diameter, 5" tall. This small basket was constructed with colorful linen cords worked in half hitches. Photograph courtesy of the artist.

(right)
Small Basket by Diane Itter. 1¼" tall, 3¼" in diameter. Notice the interest created by changing the direction of the half hitches of linen cord. Photograph courtesy of the artist.

NON TRADITIONAL BASKET TECHNIQUES

Round Start

To make a basket by this method, begin by tapering the end of the jute to a point with scissors. How far it is tapered depends upon the diameter of the jute. The heavier the jute, the longer the taper. Thread your needle with approximately one yard of yarn. Place the end of the yarn at the beginning of the taper. Hold it in place with your thumb nail. Wrap the yarn around the jute, going back over the end that you are holding. Pull tightly to secure. Wrap the yarn around the jute to the end of the taper. Curl this wrapped portion around to form a tiny circle and secure it by a wrap of yarn. Pull tight. Wrap over again. Pull tight. This beginning step may take several tries. It takes practice to manipulate the cord and yarn. Your goal is to have a neat, small round start with an opening just large enough for the needle to pass through.

Round start using raffia over reed.

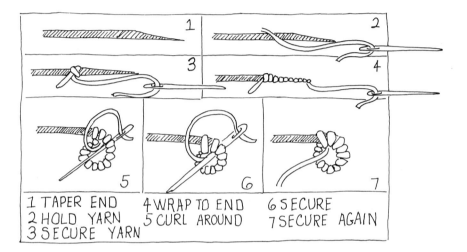

1 TAPER END
2 HOLD YARN
3 SECURE YARN
4 WRAP TO END
5 CURL AROUND
6 SECURE
7 SECURE AGAIN

Figure Eight Stitch

The figure eight stitch may be the most popular of the coiling techniques. It is strong and can be used when the rows are to blend together without the joining stitch showing. To make the figure eight stitch bring the yarn over the foundation cord, under and over the previous row, and then back under the foundation cord. For a very tight, firm surface it is best to make every stitch a figure eight stitch. However, a faster method for creating a strong surface is to make one to three wraps around the foundation cord between the figure eight stitches. Try both ways on your sample piece for many rows until you feel comfortable with them. Then move on to the next technique.

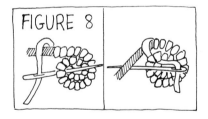

FIGURE 8

Figure eight surface using yarn over jute.

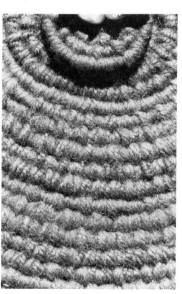

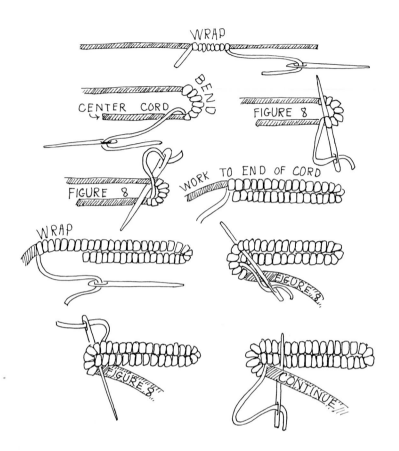

Oval start using raffia over reed.

Oval Start

Make an oval or canoe-shaped sampler by using the same materials as you would for the round start. If you are interested in making an oval basket of a specific size, the size of the finished basket must be considered before starting. To determine the length of the center cord of the base of the basket, subtract the desired width from the desired length. For example, if the finished basket base is to be three inches by five inches, the center cord will be two inches. Measure about two inches from the end of the jute. This is where the jute will be bent. Wrap around this area of the jute and tuck in the end as you do with the round start. Wrap about one-half inch of jute, depending on how heavy the jute and the yarn are. Heavy jute and yarn will require more wrapping. Now, make a bend in the middle of this wrapped area. With the needle and yarn make figure eights, back and forth, down the length of these two cords. Pull firmly as you bring the yarn over and under the cords. When reaching the end of the center cord length, continue wrapping the yarn around the cord until there is enough wrapped cord to bend around the end of the center cord, starting a new row or coil. Start making figure eights again, only this time the yarn will be going over the center cord which has already been covered with yarn. When you reach the end of the row, the beginning of your oval basket is complete.

1.

2.

1.
Soft Leather Basket by Betty Jo McDonald. 6″ in diameter, 4″ tall. Scraps of leather coil loosely around a jute foundation.

2.
Peacock Basket by Carole Lee. 3″ tall, 9″ in diameter. Wool wrapping material has been coiled over a jute foundation cord. It has been finished with a peacock feather that was split in half. Small glass beads line the perimeter.

3.

3.
Lichen Basket by Carole Lee. 7″ tall, 10″ in diameter. The wrapping material is jute used on a jute foundation cord. The basket was constructed with the figure eight and mariposa stitches. Lichens and looped yarn are sewn on after the basket is completed.

4.
Grey Basket by Carole Lee. 5″ tall, 5″ in diameter. The wrapping material is grey and black wool over a jute foundation cord. The beads and loops were attached after completion.

5.
Small Basket by Carole Lee. 4″ tall, 4″ in diameter. Brown, grey and white wool, chenille and rattail were wrapped over a jute foundation cord. The stitches used in the construction are the lazy squaw, mariposa, and the figure eight.

4.

5.

1.

Medusa by author. 4" tall, 4" wide, 4" long. Coiled raffia around a reed foundation cord. The face is made of nylon stocking stuffed with cotton with stitched features. The snakes are pipe cleaners wrapped with raffia.

2.

Coiled hat by author. 8" tall, 12" in diameter. Synthetic yarn was wrapped around soft cotton foundation cord in the figure eight and mariposa stitch. The feathers are attached on coils with wire reinforcing them.

3.

Cuckoo Basket by author. 8" tall, 13" in diameter. This basket was coiled with synthetic yarn around a jute foundation cord reinforced with wire. The figures are coiled linen around jute foundation cord, and the faces are made of nylon stocking stuffed with cotton and have stitched features.

4.

Shi-lo Basket by author. 6" tall, 13" in diameter. Raffia wrapped around a reed foundation cord makes this a stiff basket. The bottom of the basket is figure eight wrapping, but the sides are made with the shi-lo stitch.

5.

Indigo Basket by author. 7" in diameter, 10" tall. Handspun wool dyed with indigo is the wrapping material, with the patterned areas created by ikat, a resist dye technique. The basket is constructed entirely with the figure eight stitch over a jute foundation cord reinforced with wire.

6.

Container for a Fetish II by Sylvia Seventy. 1¼" wide, ¾" tall. This basket is coiled around an abalone shell with raffia around a waxed linen foundation. It has been decorated with small turquoise colored glass beads.

1.

4.

2.

5.

3.

6.

Shi-lo surface using raffia over reed.

Shi-Lo Stitch

Shi-lo means that two foundation cords are used in the basket construction; one is large and the other is small. This figure eight variation may be worked into a round or an oval basket. If making an oval piece, start the additional smaller foundation cord at the curve after the oval start is complete. Taper the end of a thinner piece of jute (smaller foundation cord) and fit it snugly between the wrapped area and the continuing foundation cord. Make three figure eights around the two foundation cords, and then attach them with a figure eight into the previous row. The shi-lo stitch is like the basic figure eight stitch in that the figure eight may work back into the previous row each time if desired. Notice that the large cord will be covered twice and the small cord will be covered once. If working on a round piece, add the new foundation cord whenever desired in the same manner as the oval. After learning this technique use it anywhere a varied surface texture is desired.

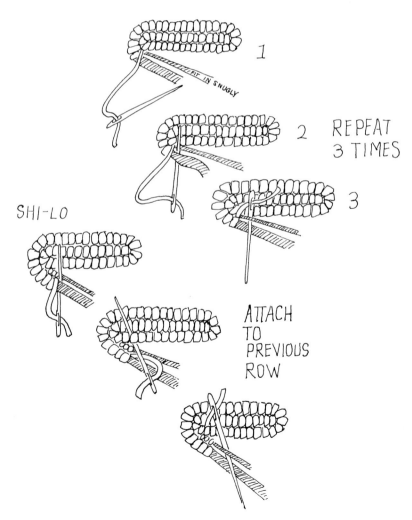

1

2 REPEAT 3 TIMES

3

SHI-LO

ATTACH TO PREVIOUS ROW

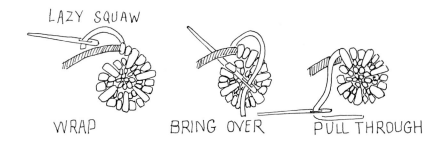

LAZY SQUAW

WRAP　　　　BRING OVER　　　PULL THROUGH

Lazy Squaw Stitch

The lazy squaw stitch is a decorative stitch which may be used in a variety of ways. With yarn, make the desired number of wraps around the foundation cord. Then, instead of joining the new row with a figure eight, just bring the needle and yarn straight down and over the previous row without the figure eight twist. Insert the needle between rows and come up on the other side. Bring the yarn over the top and wrap the foundation cord again. It should look the same on both sides. Repeat this process.

The lazy squaw stitch may be used in a "hit or miss" manner, but it is also effective when used in a well planned pattern by itself or combined with the figure eight stitch. The number of times the yarn is wrapped around the foundation cord before it is attached with the lazy squaw stitch governs the pattern. It may be not wrapped at all or may be wrapped three or four times, depending upon your materials and the "look" you wish to achieve. Always count the wraps, and be consistent to achieve an effective pattern.

The lazy squaw is not as strong as the figure eight. Try not to use it alone where strength is needed—for example, where the basket first turns up to form the sides. The materials used will also govern how the lazy squaw may be used. As with the other techniques, practice this one on your sample piece using jute and yarn before trying materials that are more difficult to handle.

Lazy squaw worked with flat reed over a round reed foundation on an old Chinese tea basket.

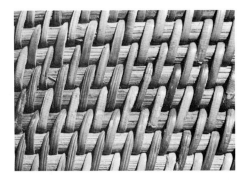

Lazy squaw worked on this basket from the Phillipines.

Mariposa or Lace Stitch

Start this "knotted looking" stitch as you would the lazy squaw. Wrap the foundation cord with yarn the desired number of times. Use your thumb to hold it and make a space between the foundation cord and the previous row. Now, as with the lazy squaw, bring the yarn down over the previous row. Bring the needle out the back, then forward in between the rows and to the left of the stitch. Now bring the needle over the stitch and insert it to the right. A knot has now been completed. At this point, wrap around this stitch again if desired. The number of times wrapped around this stitch will determine how large the separation will be between the two rows and how large the knot will appear. The type of material used will also affect this. Proceed to the next stitch by bringing the needle and yarn up over the foundation cord and repeat the process.

The mariposa, like the lazy squaw stitch, can be used to create interest. It gives a lacy look if used row after row. It may be used as a finish or as an accent on a border. Depending on the materials used, it may or may not be strong enough for use in any area of the basket. This pretty stitch will become lost when using a loosely spun material, so use it only where it will be effective, because it is time consuming.

Lace stitch and wrapping worked with a flat fiber over a round foundation cord. This type of work is done in Mexico and in the People's Republic of China. Courtesy of Lydia Van Gelder.

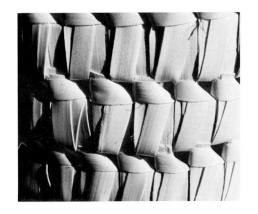

Lace stitch worked with a flat fiber over a flat fiber foundation.

Lace stitch and pattern are worked into this burden basket from South Africa. A thin fiber, twisted like rope, is worked over a large foundation. Courtesy of Basket Bazaar, Yountville, California.

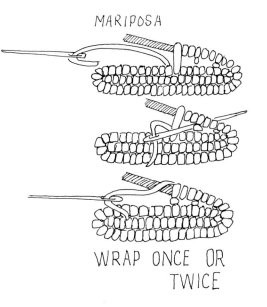

MARIPOSA

WRAP ONCE OR TWICE

1.
Feather Holder by Judy Sohigian.
6″ in diameter, 2″ tall. This feather
container was made of handspun
reindeer wool, which was coiled
over a jute foundation cord.

2.
Basket by Lisa Wagner. 12″ tall,
19″ in diameter. The foundation of
this coiled basket is made with
cotton fabric stuffed with cotton
welt cord. The fabric has been tie-
dyed with procion dyes in shades
of salmon to white. The wrapping
material is a thin mohair yarn coiled
with the lazy squaw stitch.

3.
Brushed Jute Basket by Gary
Trentham. 16″ in diameter, 9″ tall.
This basket was coiled of jute, the
surface material (jute) was added
with the knots, then unplied and
brushed. Photograph by David
Arky.

4.
Twisted Paper Basket by Gary
Trentham. 25″ in diameter, 12″ tall.
Coiled paper with twisted ends
create the surface of this basket.
Photograph by David Arky.

5.
Basket by Dolly Curtis. 10″ tall, 5″
in diameter. This basket has been
coiled with the figure eight stitch,
and raffia has been used for the
foundation and for the wrapping
material. The raffia has been dyed
with an onion skin dyebath, using
alum and tin as the mordants. Photograph courtesy of the artist.

1.

2.

3.

4.

5.

Coiled basket by Sue Cole. 3½" in diameter, 3" tall. This basket was coiled with the lazy squaw stitch of wool and mohair in grey and white. Photograph courtesy of the artist.

Adding Wrapping Material and Foundation Cord

To add more wrapping material, thread the needle with a new piece of yarn, about one yard in length, and lay the end along side of the foundation cord, together with the end of the former yarn. Hold the yarns and cord in place with your thumb and begin wrapping around the foundation cord by first wrapping over the yarn ends to secure them. Continue as before.

Add new foundation cord by tapering to a point the ends of both the original cord and the cord being added. Then place these tapered ends together and hold them in place while working into the basket. If working with very stiff material that is difficult to control, tie the ends together with sewing thread before continuing.

ADDING YARN

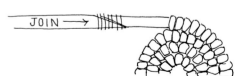

JOIN →

18   COILING

Shaping

The round or oval sample piece can become the base of a basket. Shaping is entirely an individual decision, and depends upon your ability to control the materials. To form the bottom of the basket, you coiled rows side by side. Now form the sides of the basket by working the coiled rows up and on top of the previous rows. The angle at which the rows are placed determines the shape. If the rows are stacked directly on top of each other, the shape will go up at a right angle with the bottom; if the rows are placed slightly to the side, the angle will be more obtuse. As you work around the basket, place your fingers inside it to guide the shaping. Various shapes are easily manipulated if worked with a firm, even tension. Even a crooked and lopsided basket may have charm.

Working with a template may help control the desired shape. Before beginning work on the sides of the basket, cut a template of the desired size and shape from cardboard. As your work progresses, hold the template alongside the basket to check the shaping.

In general, if the outside of the basket is to be the side that is visible, as in upright baskets, work on the outside closest to you. If the inside of the basket is to be seen, such as in bowl or tray shapes, work on the inside opposite you. These approaches are the most comfortable ways to work, and the stitching is usually neater on the side of the basket which is worked.

Before starting you should have an idea of the shape your basket will take. The materials used help determine this shape and give character to the basket. However, if necessary, materials may be adjusted to accomodate your design. For instance, if working your sample piece of yarn and jute into a basket, the basket may not hold its shape well if it gets too large. In this case, the materials may be adjusted by reinforcing the jute foundation cord with wire. Simply include the wire with the foundation cord as you wrap. Use wire or any other material that is pliable and strong in a size that seems appropriate for the other materials you are using. If using large yarn and jute on a large shape, use large wire. Use whatever is needed to give enough strength. You need only run the wire along with the jute foundation cord in the places where the direction of the basket changes. If you feel you are not getting enough body into the piece this way, use wire more often. Reed may also be used in this manner. Do whatever seems to work for you. Adding wire is only one way to adjust the materials.

After a little practice you will realize that coiling can take on any shape or direction. The basket need not start as the traditional round or oval shape. Squares and rectangles may be tried as well as a combination of shapes.

Hands holding template.

Coiling may be worked in many directions. *Holey Basket* by author.

Circular Convex Coiled Wall Hanging by Joan Michaels Paque. 36" in diameter. This piece was coiled with red and black yarns in figure eight stitches. Commissioned and purchased by Belding Lily, Shelby, North Carolina. Photograph by Henry P. Paque.

Bold color change in planned pattern areas. *Oreo Basket* by Carole Lee.

Patterns

Some of the ways to create pattern are by changing the stitch, the texture, or the color of the wrapping material. To create a subtle pattern change, use wrapping material with a different texture, but of the same color. For example, if you have been using a beige wool for wrapping material, switch to a beige rayon chenille material. The change from the dull wool to the shiny chenille will create interest. Another way to achieve a subtle pattern, without changing the color, is to use the lazy squaw stitch in a planned pattern area.

Bolder patterns are made by changing color. Make plans before you begin. Do you want a planned pattern or a hit and miss design? Add new color in the same manner as adding any new wrapping material. If you want the original color to reappear, you may carry it along with the foundation cord as you wrap with the new color. Count the number of times you wrap the new color before joining it to the previous row. Because the new row is of a contrasting color to the preceding row, the joining stitch will show. This may or may not be suitable to your pattern. If you do not want this connection to show, do not make the figure eight stitch, just pick up a piece of yarn from the previous row as you wrap.

When you want the original color to reappear, run the new color along the foundation cord, and begin wrapping with the original color.

Another technique for changing color pattern is to totally or partially cover the original color of the previous row with a new color. With a new color, make figure eight stitches every stitch with no wrapping between. The previous row of the original color will be covered. This technique may be varied with areas of solid wrapping between the solid figure eight areas.

These are just a few ways of creating pattern change. You will find more ways to create patterns while you experiment. Take any liberties with the basic techniques to achieve the results you desire.

LAZY SQUAW
PATTERN

PICK
UP
YARN

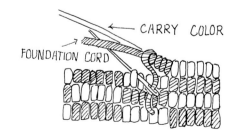

CARRY COLOR

FOUNDATION CORD

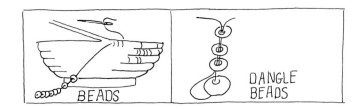

Finishes

Fur presents an excellent finish; it gives a soft texture and is easy to use. Cut the fur into strips with a single-edged razor blade. Cut on the back of the pelt with very light pressure so the blade will not cut through to the fur. You will need strips about the width of the foundation cord. Carry the strip along with the foundation cord. Wrap the cord less often when carrying fur because the wrapping will cover the fur. As you make the figure eight, some of the fur will pull under the yarn. When the stitch is completed the fur can be pulled out with the tip of a tapestry needle.

When attaching *beads,* thread them on any strong, but thin, string. This string will not show when the beads are in place. Knot the last bead on the string to hold them all secure. Tie the other end of the string to the foundation cord near where you are wrapping. Wrap the foundation cord and bead string with wrapping material until you want a bead to appear. Slide a bead up the string into position next to the foundation cord. Continue wrapping the foundation cord and bead string until you want another bead to appear.

Dangling beads are done in a similar manner. Secure one end of strong string to the foundation cord. Wrap the foundation cord and string with wrapping material until you reach the place where the beads will hang. Thread three or four beads on the string, go around the bottom bead and thread back up through the top beads. Continue to wrap around the foundation cord and string until you want more beads to appear.

Fur and beads worked with yarn over a jute foundation. *New Basket* by author.

Picaci shells held in place by fishing line. *Ikat Basket* by Lydia Van Gelder.

Beads and shells attached to basket of raffia over reed. The round shells are sewn into a wrapped foundation of several small reeds. *Shi-lo Basket* by author.

Don't Put all your Baskets in One Egg by Jessica Scarborough. These tiny baskets are coiled with silk buttonhole twist over a linen foundation in the lazy squaw stitch. Photograph by Alex Brown.

Waxed Linen Basket by Gary Trentham. 34" in diameter, 7" tall. A coiled form of linen was used for this basket. The smooth shag effect around the perimeter was achieved with linen yarn. Photograph by David Arky.

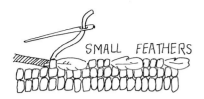

SMALL FEATHERS

The use of *feathers* can provide an elegant finish, or may add a comical look to your basket. The effect you create is determined by the feather itself, and by the way it is attached. The size of the feathers, where they are to be attached, and the wrapping material all determine how they will be secured to the basket. Small feathers may be set in place and held securely by tightly wrapping the end of the feathers in place with the wrapping material. This method will work when the feathers are small, the wrapping material is not slick, and the wrapping tension is tight enough.

Feathers give a whimsical look to the top of this coiled hat by the author.

INSIDE   BEND

MEDIUM FEATHERS   1

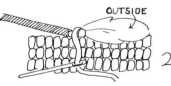

OUTSIDE   2

A medium sized feather will need a different application so that it will not pull out once it is attached. Place the feather right side in, on top of the foundation cord with the quill pointing to the right. Wrap around the quill two or three times. Make a figure eight stitch to attach to the previous row. Bend the feather a little to the left of this figure eight stitch. Fold it to the right so that the top of the feather is now on the outside. Firmly wrap the remainder of the quill an additional two or three times, then repeat the figure eight. The front of the feather is now showing and is tucked firmly into place.

Feathers frame a small mirror set into the lid of this basket made by the author.

Feathers on this lid point down-
ward after being stitched in place.
Medusa by author.

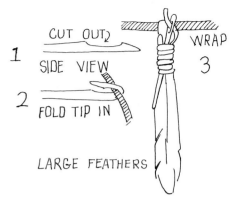

Large feathers with large hollow quills
are attached using another technique.
Place the feather on the table right side
down. With a single-edged razor blade, cut
a canoe-shaped section out of the end of the
quill. Place yarn over this cut, fold the
feather over the yarn, and place the tip of
the quill into the hollowed area. Then wrap
the quill with wrapping material. One end
of the wrapping material is tucked in and
hidden by the wrapping, the other end is
brought under the wrapping material by a
tapestry needle. Now the yarn holding the
feather may be carried along and wrapped
with the foundation cord. A similar
method is used to attach the beads.

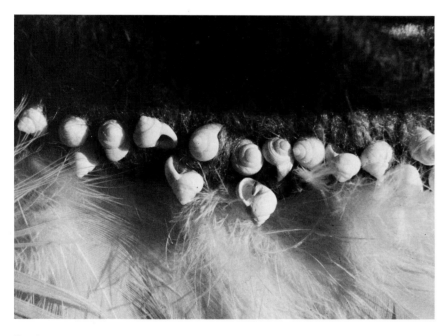

Feathers and picaci shells give an
elegant feeling to this *Ikat Basket*
made by Lydia Van Gelder.

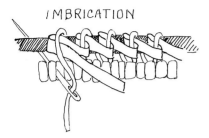

IMBRICATION

Imbricated surface on basket lid from Ethiopia. Courtesy Basket Bazaar, Yountville, California.

The *imbrication* technique was used by the Klikitat Indians. Imbrication is a method of adding color and texture to the outside of the basket. Choose a material the approximate width of the foundation cord. Secure this overlay material to the foundation cord by wrapping it with your wrapping material. Then fold the attached overlay material and stitch it firmly into place with a wrap of the wrapping material, while joining it to the previous row. This is done by slipping the needle through the top of a stitch from the previous row. Again fold the overlay material back and stitch in place. Repeat this process.

Grosgrain ribbon works well for a sampler on this small basket.

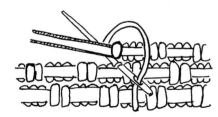

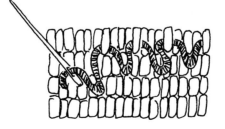

Another way of achieving an imbricated looking surface is to *lay on* another piece of material over the coiled surface. Again use a strip of material about the width of the foundation cord and secure it in place by wrapping. After the material is secure, pull the overlay material out of the way, and wrap around the foundation cord. Do not include the overlay material in this wrapping. Continue to wrap the foundation cord and secure this overlay material while joining this new row to the previous row. Join these rows with a figure eight stitch or by picking up one stitch from the previous row, as you pass the needle around. Some

of the overlay material will show and some will be hidden. The number of times you wrap it will determine the pattern. The overlay material may be laid flat against the basket surface or it may be pulled away to form loops. Another way of securing the overlay material is to wait until the basket is completed, then stitch it into place with a tapestry needle.

COILING   **27**

Balloon Basket by Kris Leedy.

Twisted Linen Basket by Gary Trentham. 7½" in diameter, 5" tall. The body of this basket has been coiled with natural linen and the surface is covered with tightly twisted knots. Photograph by John Creel.

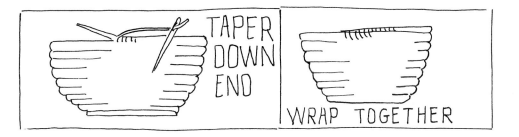

Finishing the Basket

Taper the end of the foundation cord to a point for about one and a half inches, depending on the thickness of the jute. Continue wrapping and attaching as you have been until you near the end of the foundation cord. Then wrap the end of the foundation cord and the previous row together. To conceal and secure the end of the yarn, draw the needle and yarn back through a few of the wrappings and cut.

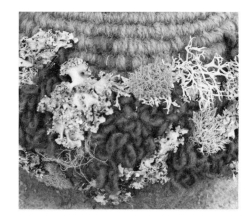

Detail of *Lichen Basket* by Carole Lee. Notice the mariposa stitch used to create the last row of this basket.

Finished last row of basket.

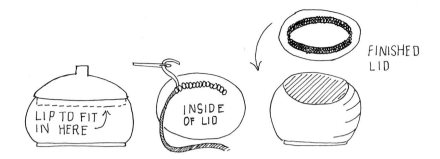

FINISHED LID

LIP TO FIT IN HERE

INSIDE OF LID

Making Lids

Some baskets seem to need a lid to make them look finished. The right lid can add character to a plain basket. Begin the lid in the same way as you did the basket and shape it as you shaped the sides of the basket. The lid may take on any shape but should complement the shape of the basket. You may work it with a large or small knob on the top, bring the sides down straight or round them out, or make the lid perfectly flat. As you are working the lid, decide how it will fit onto the basket. Will it rest slightly inside the top of the basket or will it fit over the edge of the basket? Do you want it to fit snugly, or just rest in place? If it is to fit snugly, it may need a lip on the inside. If this is the case, work the lid to fit over the edge of the basket. Finish it in the same manner that the basket was finished.

If a lip is wanted, judge where it must be worked in order for the lip to be just inside the top of the basket when the lid is on. To start the lip, using the same materials as in the basket and lid, place the foundation cord in the proper place on the inside of the lid. Wrap around the cord with wrapping material two or three times and then secure it to the lid of the basket by bringing the needle and wrapping material up through the lid and then down again. Continue wrapping and securing. You may work around to form as many rows as you wish. Usually two complete times around will be enough, depending upon your materials. Finish the lip in the same place you started, as in finishing a basket.

Lip on inside of lid will hold lid in place.

Large coiled basket by Kathy Woods. 7" tall, 12" wide, 16" long. The foundation material is jute, with caning to give it support. The wrapping material is mostly an oatmeal colored knitting worsted yarn wrapped with the figure eight stitch. The figure eight stitch was made for each stitch.

Coiled basket by Lida Gordon. 7" tall, 14" in diameter. Linen was wrapped around a jute foundation cord. Photograph courtesy of the artist.

Synthetic Basket by Barbara Goldberg. 5½" tall, 9½" in diameter. A synthetic yarn was used as the wrapping material and jute as the foundation material. Each coil begins and ends with exposed jute ends. Photograph courtesy of the artist.

Cacoon Basket, by Lisa Wagner. 2½' tall, 20" in diameter. The foundation of this coiled basket is silk fabric stuffed with a cotton welt cord. Raw silk has been used on the outside, with China silk dyed with procion dyes on the inside. The fabric was wrapped around the cotton cord as the coiling progressed. The wrapping material is handspun tussah silk yarn.

TWINING

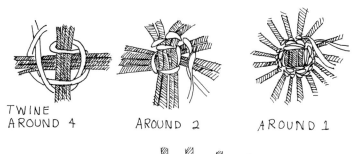

TWINE
AROUND 4   AROUND 2   AROUND 1

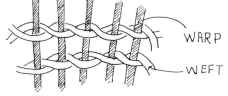

WARP

WEFT

In twining, as in coiling, there are two elements. The warp forms the structure of the basket, and the weft fills in. The warp should be strong, stiff, and have body to it, while the weft should be pliable. The materials used for the coiling sampler are also recommended for a twining sampler. There are several materials that are ideal to work with because they are easy to handle. Jute or sisal rope may be used for the warp and yarn for the weft. A yarn like rug wool has good body and will not stretch or fray while being worked. Some of the twining techniques such as lattice twining and the ti-band will work more easily with a rigid warp material. Reed twined with raffia is an excellent choice for working these techniques. After you study these basics, you will want to use your imagination and try various materials.

Beginning Twining

Start by cutting eight pieces of warp, each at least 12 inches in length. Since these pieces of warp cannot be lengthened later, they should be cut the total length of the desired basket—from the top rim of one side around the bottom to the top rim on the other side. Take four pieces of warp and cross them with the other four pieces of warp. Put their centers together. Cut a piece of yarn, at least a yard in length, for the weft. Fold it in half around one group of four warp lengths as you see in the illustration. Begin twining. Plain twining is done by weaving the two weft ends in and out of the warps. The yarn (or weft) on the inside passes to the outside, and the yarn (or weft) on the outside moves inside. Twine completely around one time, twining four warps together at once. Then twine completely around, twining two warps together at a time. Now, twine around each warp individually.

There are many ways of starting a twined basket. The following technique is simple and is often used on contemporary baskets. Cut eight warp lengths, at least 12 inches in length, and place them in two groups of four. Also cut two weft yarns, at least a yard in length. Working one group of warp lengths at a time, line them up in a row and, in the center of the lengths, weave a weft yarn in an over one, under one pattern.

Pack the yarn together firmly and weave until the length of the woven part is about equal to the width of the four warps. You will have a woven square. Now do the same with the other group of four warps. Put these two groups of warps together so that they form a cross and so that the two long ends of the weft come together at one corner. The short ends may be sandwiched between the two pieces of weaving. Begin twining with the two long ends, a process that was described in the preceding paragraph.

This start of a basket was worked with palm.

Worked with willow, this start was not made according to the directions in the chapter. The first row twines around four warps at a time, and the next and succeeding rows twine around one warp at a time.

Adding New Warp

As you twine you will notice your sampler will soon begin to "cup up" and will not lie flat. More warp lengths are needed to resolve this problem. Adding more lengths is simple; it is important to add them evenly around your work so that it will not become lopsided. To add, cut another piece of warp and bend it in the center. Slip this bend in between two existing warps. Twine around these two new warps and continue twining. Add other warps as they are needed. If you want a basket with a large flat bottom, many new warps will need to be added until the desired size is reached. When you stop adding, the shape will begin to work upward, forming the sides of the basket.

Another way to add new warp is to place a single warp into a space between two existing warps. Although this way is not as secure as bending the warp, it may be necessary if the warp material you are using will not bend in half.

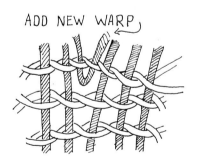

ADD NEW WARP

This twined basket is from the Philippines.

This twined basket is of kelp.

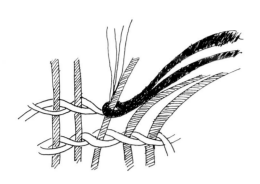

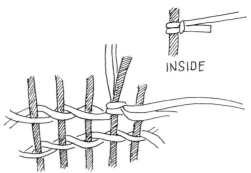

Adding New Weft

Place the short ends of the original weft material along one of the warps. Wrap the new piece of weft material around this warp, including the short ends of the original weft. Continue twining. As you twine around the basket, continue to twine around this warp and the original weft ends.

There is another method of adding weft that makes the new weft material hold securely and easy to handle. Place the short ends of the original weft material along one of the warps. With a half hitch knot, attach the new weft material over this warp and the original weft ends. This technique may be used for easily adding one or two new weft materials. If adding one new weft material, tie the knot so that there is one long end and one short end to the new weft material. Then work the short end of the new weft along with the long one as you twine. Push the rows down snugly so the addition of the new material will not be visible.

Here is a basket start of yarn and jute.

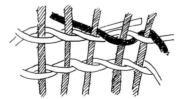

A third way of adding new weft material is to leave the short end of the weft hanging inside the basket and to lay the new material in its place. Continue twining. After another row or two has been completed, the ends may be hidden by working them under the weft with a tapestry needle or a crochet hook.

Fly Like a Bird by Judy Sohigian. 10″ tall, 6″ in diameter. Natural, brown, and beige raffia are twined over reed to spell out "fly like a bird."

Variation of Plain Twining

A way of adding interest to plain twining is to change the direction of the twist to the weft. If the direction is changed with each row of twining, it will give the overall appearance of knitting.

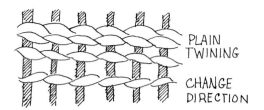

PLAIN TWINING

CHANGE DIRECTION

Twining with yarn over jute shows change in the direction of twining.

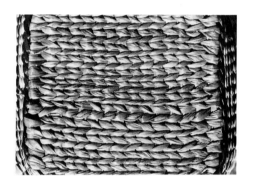

A change of twining direction is shown on the bottom of this basket from The People's Republic of China.

Twined basket by Alice Lassiter. 9" tall, 10" in diameter. Black raffia and copper wire twine over a stiff sisal foundation. The ends of the sisal have been finished by unraveling.

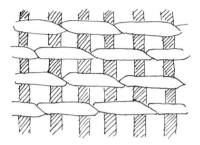

Diagonal Twining

Instead of twining around one warp at a time, twine around two warps at a time. As you twine, each succeeding row will twine around alternating warps, and it will give the appearance of a diagonal weave. The rows are twined closely together.

Diagonal twining is shown on this sample piece of yarn over jute.

Twined hat by Reuven Benjuhmin. 8" in diameter, 5" tall. Raffia, dyed with walnut hulls, and sea grass twine around reed to form this hat/basket.

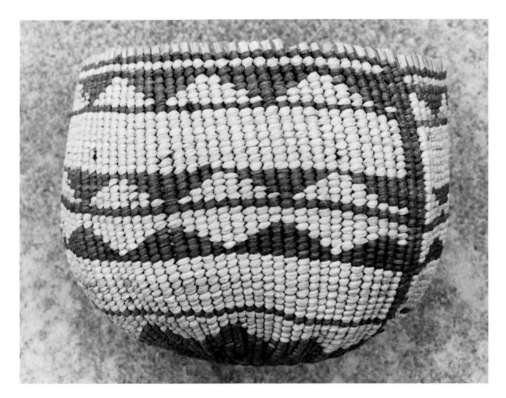

Twined basket by Bertha Carley. 5" in diameter, 4" tall. Natural raffia, some dyed with walnut hulls, twines over small reed.

Twined basket by Lynn Cannon. 7″ tall, 5″ in diameter. Plain and ti-band twining with leather strips over reed in addition to glass beads gives this basket an American Indian look.

Twined basket by Nancy Bess. 9½″ tall, 6″ wide. Cotton cord is twined over manilla rope with frayed ends. Photograph by Steve Anderson.

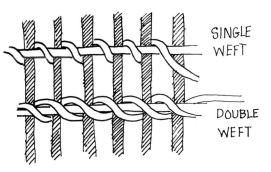

SINGLE WEFT

DOUBLE WEFT

Ti-band and Wrapped Twining

This technique adds another weaving element and strengthens the basket. While giving a three-dimensional appearance to the outside of the basket, the inside continues to look like plain twining. The addition of an extra weaving band can look very ornamental on the sides of a basket. This band may be covered completely by *ti-band* twining with two weft elements or the band may be left partially exposed by wrapped twining with only one weft element. If a band of a new color is introduced, an interesting texture will be achieved. These rows of bands may be placed close together for a solid area or they may be spaced apart.

Cut a piece of warp material for the band. Jute will be satisfactory, but a stiffer material may be easier to work. Try reed or sisal rope for the band. Hold it horizontally on the outside of the warps and twine it into place. The twining procedure is the same as with plain twining, with the exception that one or two weft elements twine around the band as well as the warp.

Ti-band and wrapped twining are on the side of this basket from Ethiopia. Courtesy of the Basket Bazaar, Yountville, California.

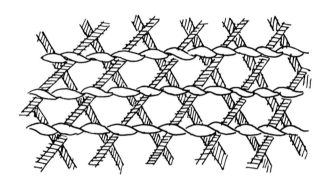

Lattice Twining or Crossed Warp Twining

This type of twining is done by the Indians of the Northwestern United States. It is a very popular technique for covering bottles or for the sides of baskets. Rigid materials, such as thin reed worked with raffia, are best for this technique. Experiment with your sampler materials on the sides of the basket to discover those which best suit your needs. Lattice twining is done by having the warps cross each other. Begin the first row by twining two warps together, crossing them as you twine, making sure that the same warp from each pair falls to the front of the other as you progress. The succeeding rows will have the same warps crossing to the front and to the back, as in the former rows. Continue in this way using the photograph as a guide for progressing from one row to the next. You may twine around the place where the warps cross, as top illustration demonstrates, or between the crosses as shown at left.

This lattice twining from the Philippines shows how to progress from one row to the next.

These two variations of lattice twining show crossing warps.

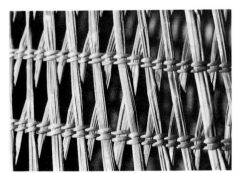

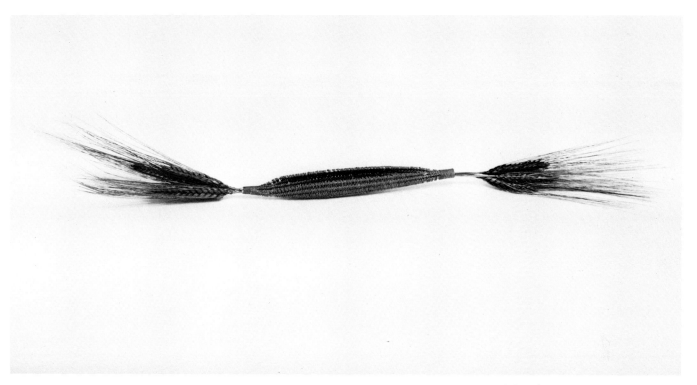

(above)
Twined basket by Nancy Bess. 26"
total length, 1" wide. Waxed linen
is twined over bearded wheat.
Photograph by Steve Anderson.

Twined basket by Nancy Bess. 16"
tall, 3½" wide. This basket is
twined with cotton cord on
bearded wheat. Photograph by
Steve Anderson.

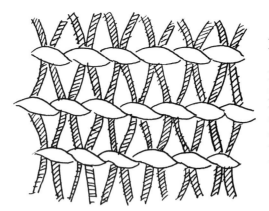

Reticulated Twining

Reticulated twining gives the appearance of lattice work, but the warps do not cross. In a manner similar to the one necessary for diagonal twining, twine around pairs of alternating warps. In reticulated twining, the warp is flexible and space is left between the rows.

RETICULATED
TWINING

Reticulated twining is on this strainer from South Africa. Courtesy of the Basket Bazaar, Yountville, California.

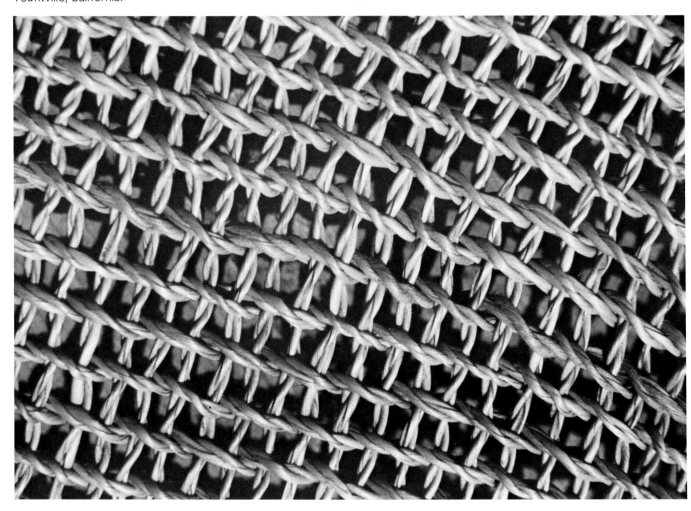

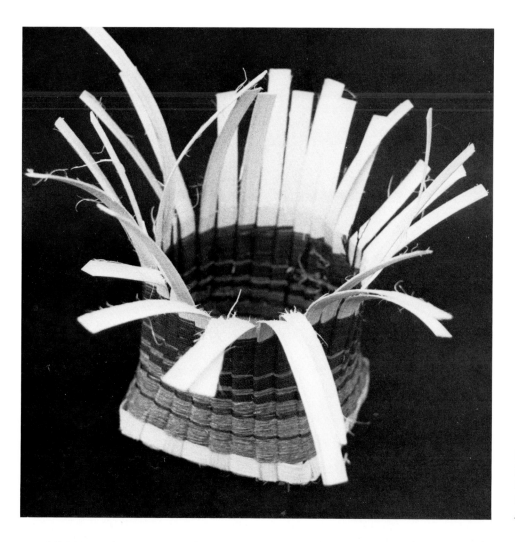

Basket in progress by B. J. Adams. 5″ square plaited bottom. Waxed linen and nylon cord twine around ½″ splints. Photograph by Clark G. Adams.

Basket in progress by B. J. Adams. Soft yarns of orange, yellow, and magenta twine around a stiff synthetic warp. Photograph by Clark G. Adams.

U-Nighted by B. J. Adams. 43" long, 19" wide, 9" deep. Video tape and plastic twined over a warp of poly-propylene form this sculpture. Photograph by Clark G. Adams.

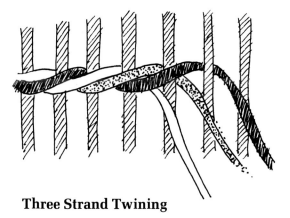

Here is an example of three strand twining of yarn over sisal.

Three Strand Twining

Twining with three strands is a way to work three colors at one time. Work with three weft materials of strong contrast. Add a third weft by laying a new piece of weft material into the space to the right of two existing weft materials. To work this technique, start with the weft material on the left. Bring it to the right and in front of two warps, then behind the third warp, and forward between the third and fourth warps. Repeat this process over and over, always working with the weft material on the left.

Wings by B. J. Adams. 9½" tall, 5" wide. This free form basket is constructed with plastic film over plastic welt cord. Synthetic yarn fringe is worked on after completion. Photograph by Clark G. Adams.

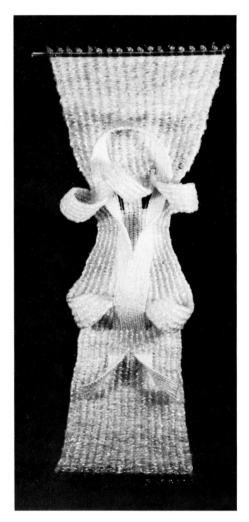

Twined Plastic Tubing Basket by
B. J. Adams. 4" in diameter, 6" tall.
Plastic tubing twines over a warp
of plastic cord. Photograph by
Clark G. Adams.

Celluloid Heros by B. J. Adams.
50" long, 24" wide, 5" deep. Twined
hanging created from plastic strips
over plastic tubes. Photograph by
Clark G. Adams.

Shaping

The shape of a twined basket does not have as much freedom as that of a coiled basket. However, shaping can be controlled by the addition or the elimination of warp. New warp may be added evenly around the basket, or added in only one area to give a lopsided or free form feeling. Warp may be eliminated as you work up the sides of the basket. Warp ends may be left exposed and be cut and frayed to benefit the design. They may also be tucked inside the basket and cut off so that they will not show. If using a pliable material, you may change the tension with which you twine to vary the shape of the basket. Changing the weft material from thick to thin, stiff to soft, will also alter the shape.

Color and Design

There are various ways to change color while twining. If twining with two colors of weft material, vertical stripes will develop. Three strand twining, with each weft of a different color, can create a spiraling movement up the sides of the basket. Horizontal stripes can be made by changing the colors for each row. The original weft color or colors may be left hanging inside the basket while working the new color, and then picked up and worked again when needed. When working a designated pattern area, add new weft materials where needed, again leaving the original ones temporarily hanging inside the basket.

Design may be created by twining some areas and not others. The direction of twining may be changed. Slits may be created. Various combinations of twining techniques may be used together. The possibilities are endless. Do some experimenting to come up with some new ideas.

This section of a belt, made of yarn over jute, shows change in the direction of twining. Note also the addition of beads and the open areas in the pattern.

BEAD   FRAY ENDS

FOLD ENDS IN

INSIDE

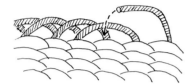

Finishes

The way the basket is finished depends upon the design and the materials used. If the basket has been woven tightly, it may be finished by simply cutting off the warp. Beads may be added to the ends of the warp. However, if the basket has been loosely woven, they may slip off. A more decorative finish may be made by fraying the ends of the warps if this technique suits your design and materials. Besides the ways suggested by the illustrations, there are a variety of ways to bring the warp ends back into the weft material where they may be completely hidden or left partially showing. You may also want to end the weft by hiding its ends inside the woven weft, alongside a warp.

This palm basket was ended by simply cutting off the warp ends.

This palm basket was ended by folding the warp ends down and weaving them back in. Then thin strips of palm were worked back over the last row. Artist, Barbara Pendola.

Leather and Spice by B. J. Adams. 14" by 9" by 8". This sculpture was created from leather, wool, and nylon twined over leather strips. Photograph by Clark G. Adams.

An Albatross Awaits by B. J. Adams. 43 " long, 12" wide. Plastic strips and polypropylene twine over a plastic welt cord to create a sculptural form. Photograph by Clark G. Adams.

They See Only Themselves (with see-thru mirror) by B. J. Adams. 5'8" total height. The warp of this twined helmet is plastic welt cord and the weft is plastic tubing. The hanging strips are braided plastic. Photograph by Clark G. Adams.

Purple-Blue Twined Basket by Gladys Weiner. 9″ tall, 9″ in diameter. A sisal weft twines over a sisal and jute warp. The opening is finished with glass beads held in place with knots. Photograph by Bob Hansen.

Basketry Form by Patricia Malarcher. 14″ long. This basket was twined with sea grass as the warp and waxed linen as the weft. Photograph courtesy of the artist.

PLAIT-ING

Hands plaiting.

Plaiting is often called braiding. As with other weaving techniques there is an overlapping of terms. Plaiting is the interlacing of flat elements. The simpler type of plaiting interlaces only two elements in a weaving over one, under one pattern. Plaiting may also be worked in more complicated patterns with three or more elements if desired.

Many items may be plaited: mats, baskets, belts, bags, to name a few. Before beginning an item such as a basket, it is wise to make a pattern on graph paper, and to work it out with strips of construction paper. As a beginning project, consider only two elements. Plan a pattern that pleases you. Even though any design or pattern may be plaited, a small repeat pattern will be easier to work than a large design. Cut strips of construction paper, making one element dark, the other light. Work out the pattern following the graph paper design exactly. Try many designs until you feel comfortable with them.

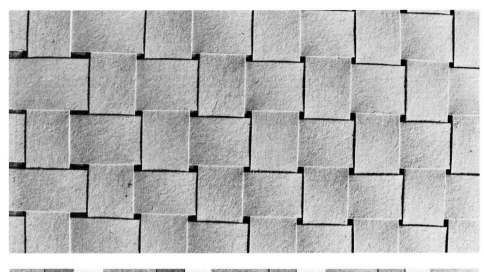

These two designs were woven with construction paper.

This section of a basket from the Philippines has been plaited with two elements. Courtesy of Basket Bazaar, Yountville, California.

(above)
Here is a section of a multi-element plaited basket from China. Courtesy of Basket Bazaar, Yountville, California.

(right)
This pattern was woven with construction paper.

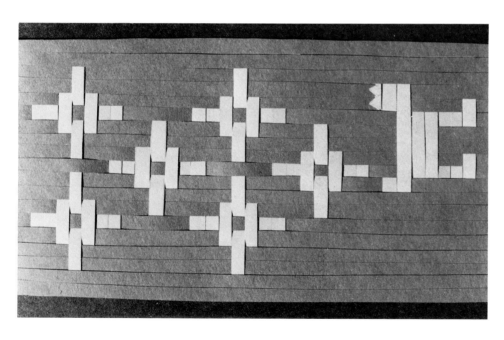

Any design may be planned on
graph paper and then plaited.

A design may be recorded on graph paper from an existing plaited piece and then may be worked into a basket. This leaf design is from a basket made about 1850 by the Miwok Indian Tribe of California. Courtesy of Lydia Van Gelder.

Sisters Basket by Marcia Floor. 8" tall, 12" wide. Plaited with leather strips, this basket has a face on both sides. Courtesy of Kathy A. Miller

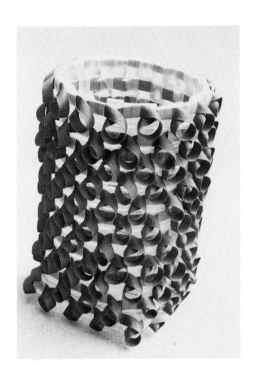

(far left)
Blue Ribbon Basket by author. 5" in diameter, 8" tall. Using plastic binding tape, this basket was first woven, then embellished with blue grosgrain ribbon in the third Algonquin technique.

(left)
Red Ribbon Basket by author. 12" tall, 9" in diameter. This basket is constructed of two grocery bags. The lower half of the basket was drawn on the bag with red felt pen to look like the woven part above. Before the weft was woven, it was wrapped with strips of red grosgrain and satin ribbon.

Twining raffia around the bottom of this basket holds it secure before the sides are constructed.

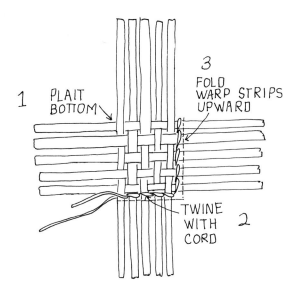

1 PLAIT BOTTOM

3 FOLD WARP STRIPS UPWARD

TWINE WITH CORD

2

The bottom of a basket is a good place for a plaited design. You may use any flat material for this basket, such as construction paper, wild materials (like palm), caning, folded newspaper strips or any flat element that interests you.

For a sample basket, cut the plaiting elements at least 12 inches long and about one-half inch wide. Begin by plaiting the bottom of the basket into the pattern. Working in the center of the strips, plait them until they reach the desired size of the bottom. A row of twining with cord or raffia around the finished bottom section will hold it secure. The extending strips will become the warps.

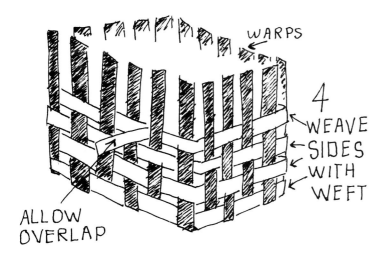

WARPS

4 WEAVE SIDES WITH WEFT

ALLOW OVERLAP

The sides of this basket may be formed with the use of a foundation such as a box or a milk carton. It may also be worked freely. If a foundation is to be used, work the bottom of the basket the same size as the bottom of the foundation; then the sides of the basket may be formed by holding them up against the sides of the foundation. The sides may be worked in the pattern or they may be plaited in a simple over and under pattern with weft strips.

The bottom of this palm basket was worked to the same size as the bottom of a milk carton. Then it was placed on the bottom of the carton; the warps were folded down over the sides of the carton and were held in place by rubber bands. The sides are formed by weaving the weft strips into place. Each weft strip should overlap it-self, about one inch, where the ends meet, then the excess should be cut off.

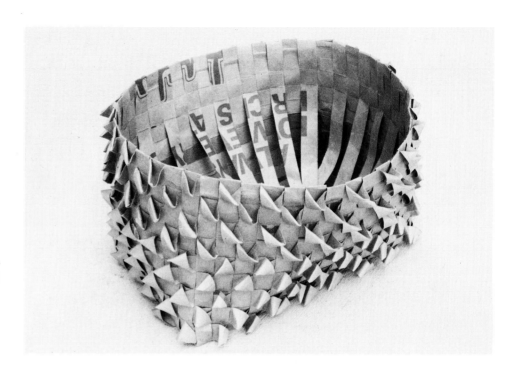

Brown Bag Basket II by author. 8″ tall, 12″ in diameter. This basket was constructed in the same manner as was Brown Bag Basket I and then embellished with the fourth Algonquin technique. The long warps were woven back into themselves on the inside of the basket and left uncut.

Brown Bag Basket I by author. 11″ tall, 12″ in diameter. Three grocery bags were used for the construction of this basket; one was used for the warp, one for the weft, and one for the surface embellishment. First, warps are cut on one large grocery bag, from top to bottom. Do not cut the bottom of the bag. Then, the wefts are cut from another grocery bag of equal size by cutting circular strips.

The warp and weft are woven together in a plain over one, under one weave and then embellished with the sixth Algonquin technique.

Pattern is only one way of making plaiting interesting; there are a variety of other techniques to consider. Weaving elements may be spaced close together or apart. They may be placed at right angles to each other, or at oblique angles. Extra elements may be "laid in" for a change in color or texture. Colors and their values may be alike or contrasting. Elements of different sizes may be used. One or both elements may be curved. The elements may be wrapped with another flat element before they are plaited together.

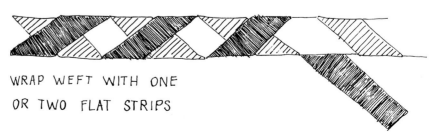

WRAP WEFT WITH ONE
OR TWO FLAT STRIPS

This angular design was woven with construction paper.

This section of a scoop was made in Taiwan. Courtesy of Basket Bazaar, Yountville, California.

These designs were woven with construction paper.

This section of a basket is from the Philippines. Courtesy of Basket Bazaar, Yountville, California.

Section of a basket from the Philippines. Courtesy of Basket Bazaar, Yountville, California.

These two color patterns were woven with construction paper.

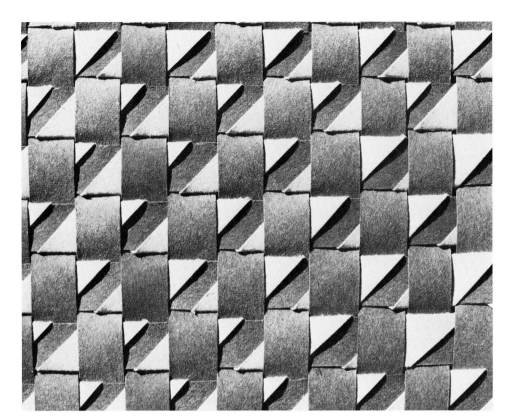

These two pieces were woven with construction paper, after the wefts were first wrapped with one (a) or two (b) strips of contrasting construction paper. This technique is found in Mexican work.

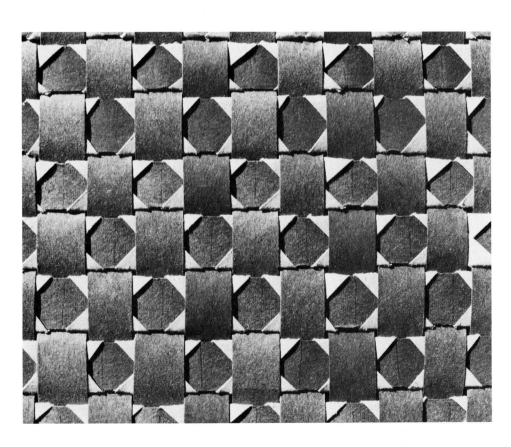

Ribbon and mylar basket by author. 4" tall, 5" in diameter. Mylar and grosgrain ribbon were woven into a plain weave to create this basket.

Black and White Print Basket by author. 11" tall, 11" in diameter. First a basket was woven using two grocery bags. The surface was embellished with strips cut from black and white photos using a plain weave, and the first and sixth Algonquin technique.

Basket by Shereen LaPlantz. 12" in diameter, 15" tall. This basket was woven in a plain weave, over one, under one. Waxed linen has been twined around the bottom and sewn around the lip. Ciba dyes have been painted on the heavy paper fiber splint to simulate the Algonquin block stamping technique. Photograph by David M. LaPlantz.

Basket by Shereen LaPlantz. 2½' across, 4" deep. This multi-element basket was plaited with paper fiber splint, flat splint reed and round reed. Waxed linen was stitched on the lip. Photograph by David M. LaPlantz.

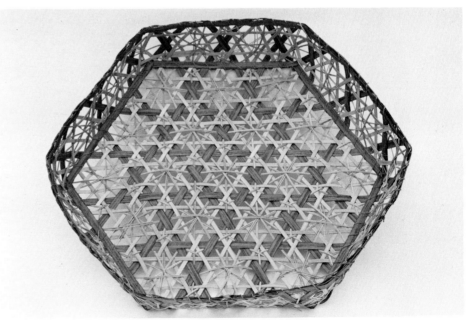

The Algonquin Techniques

The Algonquin techniques, named after the North American Indian Tribes of Canada and the Great Lakes region, offer interesting surface embellishments for plaited baskets. There are six of these techniques, most of which are made by a simple twist of a flat element. It is a good idea to practice these techniques with a material that is easy to handle, such as grosgrain ribbon. Make a sampler using cardboard, strong cord, and ribbon. Notch the top and the bottom of the cardboard with a knife, about every one-half inch. Make a warp by threading the notches from top to bottom with the cord. Practice these six techniques using the cord to hold the ribbon in place.

The first technique requires no twist of the ribbon. Simply slide the ribbon under the warp, pulling it up between the warp cords. The same side of the ribbon is always on top.

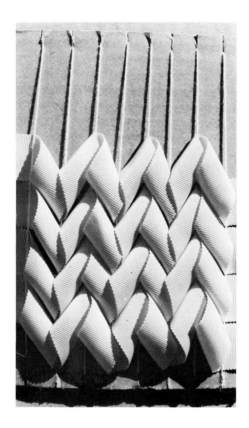

This sampler is made of cardboard and grosgrain ribbon.

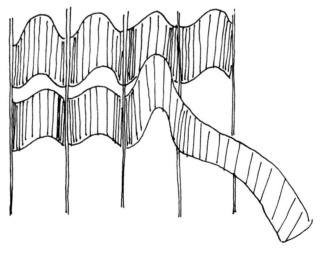

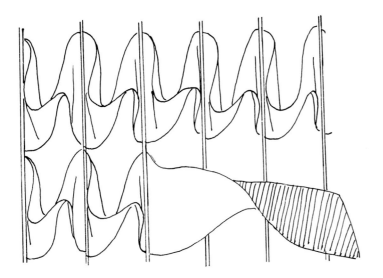

The second technique makes a twist that creates a point. As a ribbon comes out from under one warp, twist it so that the reverse side of the ribbon is now on the surface. Then insert it under the next warp.

The third technique is made by rolling the ribbon around your finger before sliding it under the next warp. The same side of the ribbon is always on top.

The fourth technique forms a curve with a point. The ribbon is folded over and down, at a right angle to the weft. The reverse side of the ribbon slides under the next warp.

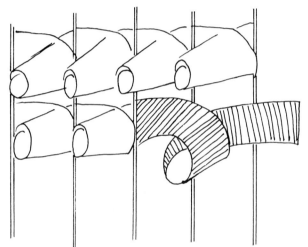
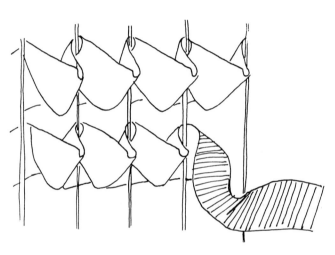

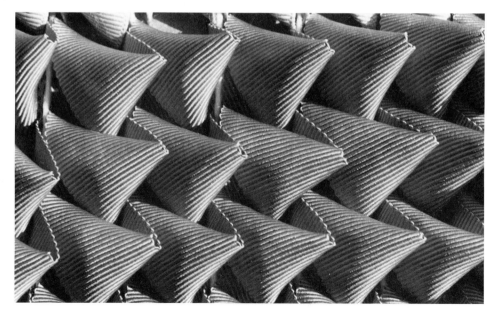

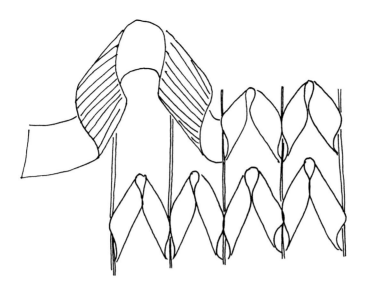

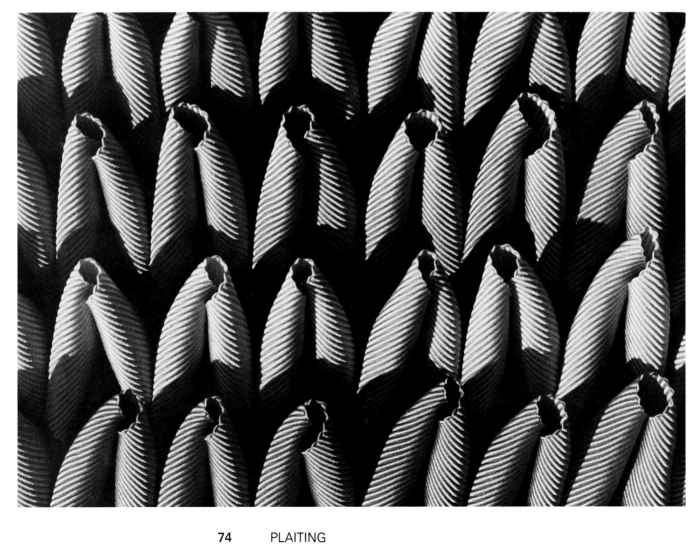

The fifth technique is formed by twisting the ribbon first in one direction and then back again, before inserting it under the next warp. The same side of the ribbon slides under the next warp.

In the sixth technique, the ribbon does not move straight across as it does in the others. It moves up and down, while moving across. The ribbon comes out from under a warp, twists over and goes down under the next warp, then twists over and goes up under the next warp. The same side of the ribbon always slides under the warp.

Once you become familiar with these techniques, you may use them on the sides of a plaited basket. One technique may be worked alone or it may be worked in combination with others. These techniques may be worked into the surface of a completed basket in a simple one over, one under pattern. Here are two baskets made by first constructing the basket shape and then adding the surface embellishment.

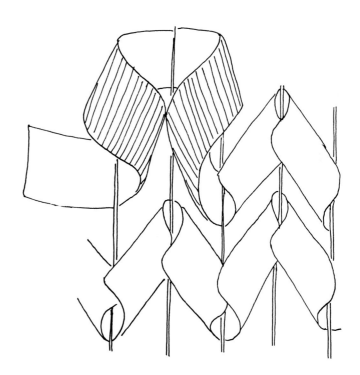

Basket by Shereen LaPlantz. 14" in diameter, 7" tall. This basket was embellished in the fifth Algonquin technique as it was woven. Waxed linen has been twined at the top to finish. Photograph by David M. LaPlantz.

Basket by Shereen LaPlantz. 2', 18", 6". Paper fiber splint woven in a plain weave with waxed linen sewn around the lip. Photograph by David M. LaPlantz.

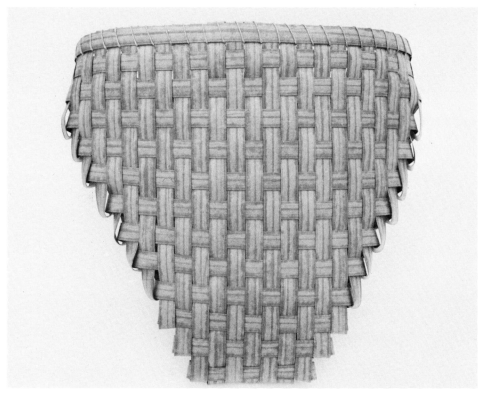

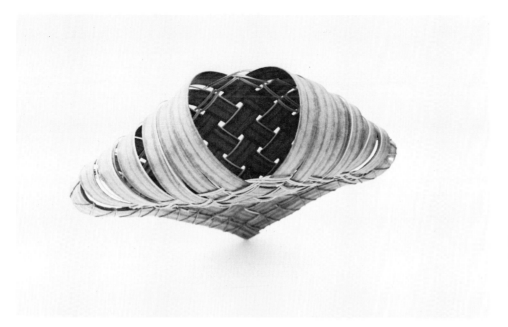

Basket by Shereen LaPlantz. 9″, 9″, 4″. Paper fiber splint and round reed were woven together, and waxed linen was sewn on the edges. Photographs by David M. LaPlantz.

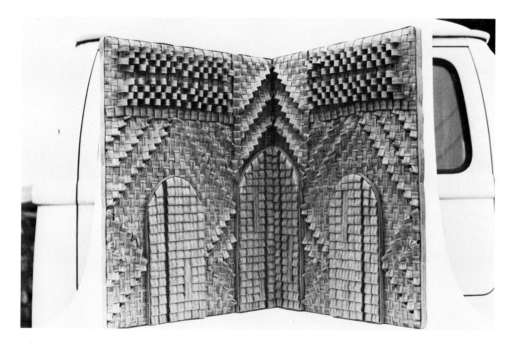

Corner Piece by Shereen LaPlantz. Each section 24″ by 18″. This piece has been imbricated, plaited, and embellished with the Algonquin and Philippine techniques. Photograph by David M. LaPlantz.

This basket, made by the Ojibway Indians of the Great Lakes region, is made of splints, some of which have been colored with vegetable dyes. This type of basket is first constructed with splints of two sizes. The warp pieces are the same size, but the weft alternates using a thick and then a thin piece in a simple over one, under one pattern. Then the ornamental strips are added to the surface. These are worked vertically. Working from the top of the basket, an ornamental strip is secured by slipping it under the left side of a basket strip or warp. It is folded forward and down, then inward and to the right, bringing it under the next basket strip and to the other side. The folding is repeated on the right side of the basket strip. Fold it forward and down, under and to the left. It now slips under a basket strip to bring it to the left side again. Repeat this process.

Ojibway basket, 5" tall, 4" diameter, purchased in Michigan in 1957. Courtesy of Helen Perks.

A grosgrain ribbon sampler.

This is a contemporary basket made in the Philippines. First the basket is constructed and then the surface embellishment is added by working strips in two directions. An ornamental strip is added by securing it in place under a basket strip. It is then twisted completely around so that the same side of the strip is now facing up again. This twisted strip then slips under the next basket strip to hold it in place. Repeat these steps. Cover the basket strips in both directions.

Philippine basket, 6" tall, 6" diameter. Courtesy of Helen Perks.

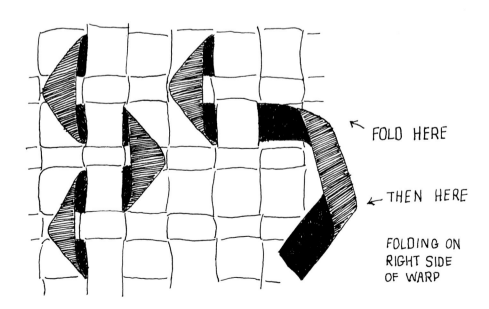

FOLD HERE

THEN HERE

FOLDING ON RIGHT SIDE OF WARP

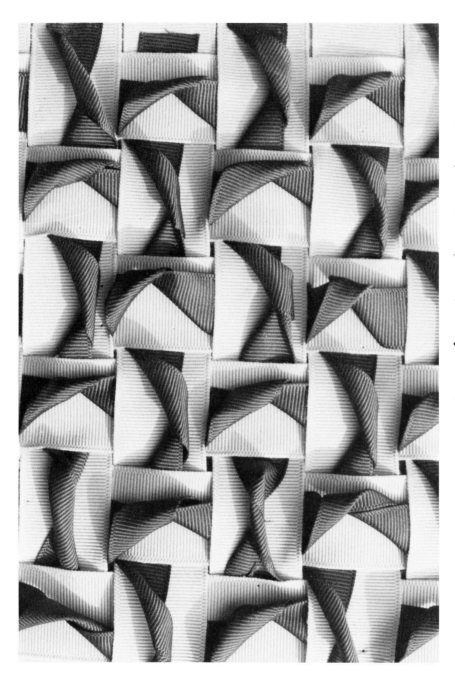

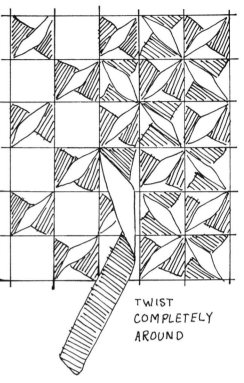

TWIST
COMPLETELY
AROUND

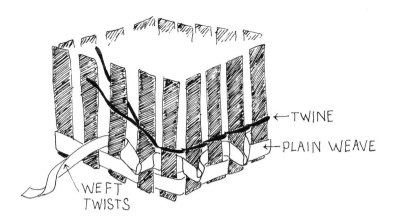

The Algonquin techniques may also be worked into a basket as it is being constructed, instead of being applied to the finished surface. In this case, the basket should be constructed of a stiff material to help it hold its shape. A row of twining is also needed between each weft to hold it securely in place. This basket has been constructed in such a way. The bottom is woven one over, one under, with twining between each row. The sides of the basket are then formed by weaving rows of weft under one warp, then over the next warp. As the weft goes over each warp, it twists before going under the next warp. After each row of weft is worked, add a row of twining with a strong material to secure the row of weft into place.

Basket by Shereen LaPlantz. 6″ tall, 6″ in diameter. This basket was embellished as it was woven according to the fifth and sixth Algonquin techniques. Waxed linen was stitched on top. Photograph by David M. LaPlantz.

A closeup of the bottom of this basket.

Basket by Shereen LaPlantz. 18" in diameter, 7" tall. This basket was first woven in a plain weave, using reed on the bottom and the top for support. Then it was embellished with the sixth Algonquin technique. Photograph by David M. LaPlantz.

Small mylar and cellophane basket by author. 6" tall, 6" wide. This basket was constructed, similar to *Mace,* and then embellished with mylar.

A detail of a place mat.

Open Weave

The open weave technique is seen on this place mat which was probably made in the Philippines. Flat elements, such as papers, wild materials, and synthetic strips are exciting materials for this technique.

This technique may be worked on a square or rectangular basket, similar to the basket shown earlier in this chapter which was formed over a box. Begin with vertical warps that are spaced apart. Lay a horizontal strip behind these vertical warps at a right angle and hold it in place by the weft strip which is wrapped around the point where the horizontal strip and vertical warps cross. Working from left to right, start the weft strip in the front, pass it over the cross and then behind at the upper right hand corner of the cross. Bring the weft strip down in the back and forward at the lower left hand corner of the cross. Repeat these motions. Continue in this way until the entire horizontal strip or first row is completely wrapped with weft. Add more rows of horizontal strips and cover them with weft strips in the same way. After all the horizontal rows are completed, begin to work the vertical rows.

This basket by the author is made of agapanthus stalk with the open weave technique. It is 6″ in diameter, 3½″ tall. The bottom is a plain over one, under one weave.

Start to weave at the top of the vertical warps with a new weft strip. Weaving through the horizontal weft strips, bring the vertical weft strip down on the right side of the cross going under one, then over one. Bring the weft strip to the back at the lower right hand corner of the cross. Then, from the back, it comes up from the lower left hand corner and crosses over the cross to the upper right hand corner. Here it goes to the front where it weaves over one, under two, over one, and then passes to the back again. Repeat this process until the vertical row is covered. Each vertical row is worked in the same manner. This weaving is done from the front side only; the reverse side is shown only to illustrate what it should look like. The vertical warps may be finished by folding them down and tucking them under weft strips. Beginning and ending weft strips may be done by tucking them under a near weft strip.

This technique may be altered to suit your needs. Depending on the materials you use and the style you choose, your basket may be woven without the foundation materials of vertical warps and horizontal strips. While these materials give strength to the weaving, they may not always be necessary. You may also work the horizontal and vertical weft strips at the same time, instead of working all the horizontal weft strips and then all the vertical weft strips. This technique is accomplished by weaving a vertical weft strip into a horizontal weft strip each time the horizontal weft strip wraps the cross.

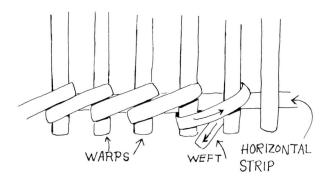

WARPS   WEFT   HORIZONTAL STRIP

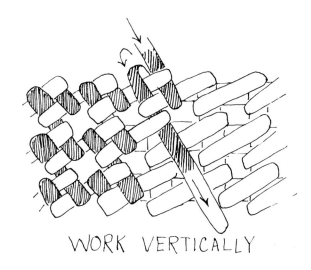

WORK VERTICALLY

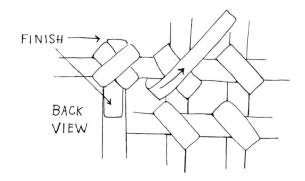

FINISH →

BACK VIEW

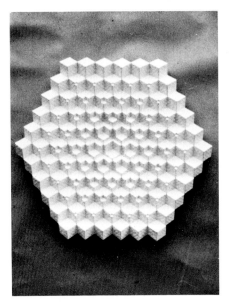

Alba Ninety-One by Earl G. Snellenberger. 42" high, 48" wide, 7" deep. Plaited of ½" wide strips of white vinyl. Photograph courtesy of the artist.

Arcturus I by Earl G. Snellenberger. 36" high, 12" in diameter at the widest point. Plaited with ¾" strips of silver mylar plastic. Photograph courtesy of the artist.

(below)
Alba Ninety-One by Earl G. Snellenberger. Detail. Photograph by Terry Taylor.

WILD BASKET MATERIALS

Wild basket materials may be found growing in your back yard, in a nearby field, marsh or woods, or on a beach. Because these materials are gathered in their natural state, they have irregularities which offer a new challenge to the basket maker who has been using commercial materials. The techniques used in making wild baskets are the same, just the "feel" of the materials and the "look" of the basket are different.

There is a large variety of wild basket materials available for use. In California there are 78 species of plants that have been used for basketry by the Indians. Learn about the plants native to your region, as well as those plants which were used by the Indians. You will discover that many parts of a plant may contribute to basket making. Stems, bark, seeds, leaves, pods, roots, shoots, branches, and sap may all be used for warp, weft, or dye materials. Wild basket making requires considerable experimentation to learn which local plants are usable, which are best for the warp or the weft, and which techniques are most suitable for these materials.

Wild materials offer a wide range of color, texture, shape, size, and firmness. Many factors affect their general appearance, such as the time of year they are picked, and the locale in which they grow. Materials may also change color after drying, soaking, or boiling; vegetable dyes will change the color of some materials. Many good books are available on the subject of vegetable or natural dyes.

The American Indians have beautifully developed their use of wild materials for basketry. They carefully preserve the natural look of wild materials and enhance the beauty of these materials by using simple designs. Contemporary basket makers can only benefit from studying such works.

(above)
Wild basket by Lucy Traber. 22" tall, 11" in diameter. This basket was twined with palm, agapanthus, and New Zealand flax.

Willow branches drying, some
with leaves removed.

Working with Wild Materials

The general requirements for wild basket materials are that the warp be rigid and strong, and the weft strong and pliable. Strength is important with any material; a weak fiber will break when it is being woven or will not endure after the basket is completed. When creating with wild materials, it is important to keep the following in mind.

GATHERING Many materials are collected when their growth is completed and they are fresh, not when they have begun to dry out or decay. Gathering seasons vary from one material to another and from one area to another.

PREPARATION Depending on the basket to be constructed, some materials may need preparation before drying, such as splitting or scraping. Sometimes cleaning the material is all that is required.

STORAGE Materials are stored in dry, cool, airy, dark, or shady places in order to preserve them in their best condition. Dampness will cause a material to rot, and too much light will cause dryness and bleaching. As wild materials dry, they shrink in size and become stiff. Some may be used fresh if a certain amount of shrinkage is desirable in the design of the basket.

USE If materials have been dried, they must be soaked to make them pliable again. Soaking them in warm water for approximately thirty minutes will make them workable. Thinner, lighter materials will take less time to soften than thicker, heavier ones. Don't soak materials longer than is necessary as this will weaken them. To keep them moist, they may be kept wrapped in a damp towel or a plastic bag while working with them. If they dry, they must be soaked again.

We will now examine ways in which various wild basket materials are prepared and used. Many of the following are particularly popular with contemporary basket makers.

Basket by Carol Hart. 2′ tall, 1¾′ wide. This wicker basket is made of weeping willow. Photograph courtesy of the artist.

Willow

You may use any of the many varieties of willow available where you live. The different species offer a wide color choice to the basket maker. Most species grow in moist soils, often near river banks.

GATHERING Choose the roots, shoots, or the thin pliable ends of the branches. Pick those that are long, thin, and straight. The young shoots are available in the springtime; spring and fall are good gathering seasons.

PREPARATION The willow may be stripped of its skin to make it white, and made smooth with a sharp edged instrument. It may be split into narrow strands. To darken willow, place it in a moistened plastic bag for a few days, and then allow it to dry thoroughly before storing. Another alternative is to simply leave the willow as it is. The contemporary basket weaver often uses the willow freshly picked, without drying, in order to show its natural beauty.

STORAGE Willow should be bundled and stored in a dry, cool, airy, and dark place.

USE If the willow has been dried, soak it for about thirty minutes in warm water to make it flexible. The Indians used willow for coiling warp and weft, and for twining warp and weft. Twining and wicker work are excellent techniques for working willow into a contemporary basket.

Cattails drying on newspaper.

Corn husks drying on newspaper.

Cattails

Cattails are found in many parts of the world. They grow in marshy places, such as around lakes, ponds, and rivers. Their availability and versatility make them an excellent plant for basket makers to use.

GATHERING It is best to pick them in the late summer when they have reached their full maturity. The green color of the leaves will have developed and the head of the cattail will be firm. Cut the leaves and stalks at the water line.

PREPARATION The stalks may be split in two with a knife and allowed to dry and bleach in the sun. After they are dry, they may be split again and again into smaller sizes. The leaves are dried whole.

STORAGE Cattails should be bundled and stored in a dry, cool, airy, and dark place.

USE Soak them in warm water for about thirty minutes to soften them before using. The Indians used cattails many ways. The leaves and stalks were split and used as warp or weft. Contemporary basket makers often use cattail leaves in twining or wicker work over a stiff warp, such as palm. The leaves, being wide and flat, will plait nicely. The leaves and stalks may be split and bundled for a coiling foundation.

Corn Husks

Any variety of corn husk may be used and may be gathered from your garden or purchased at the supermarket.

GATHERING Save the husks from corn as you prepare it for a meal.

PREPARATION Separate the husks from the silk and spread them on newspaper to dry.

STORAGE After drying, the corn husks may be bundled and then stored in a dry, cool, airy, and dark place.

USE Soak them in warm water until pliable. They may be split and bundled for coiling foundations or they may be opened flat and used for twining or plaiting.

Braided Cattail Basket by Dorothy Gill Barnes. 18″ diameter, 14″ tall. The braided cattail leaves are woven together and tied with lily braids. Photograph courtesy of the artist.

Iris leaves.

Dried and bundled palm.

Iris

Iris leaves also offer availability and versatility to the basket maker. Many varieties of iris, wild or cultivated, are available.

GATHERING Gather iris leaves when they have dried and turned shades of brown, usually in the late fall.

PREPARATION Clean dirt off the leaves and spread them on newspaper to dry any moisture.

STORAGE After they are thoroughly dry, the leaves should be bundled and stored in a dry, airy, cool, and dark place.

USE Soak the leaves for about thirty minutes in warm water to soften. They may be split or left whole. They may be used for foundation or wrapping material in coiling, and for twining, wicker work, or plaiting.

Palm

Palm is found mostly in tropical areas, however a few types are found in the more temperate zones. It is an excellent material because it is both strong and pliable. It adapts to many shapes and may be used in decorative as well as utilitarian basketry. Many varieties of palm may be used.

GATHERING Palm may be cultivated at any time. Because you pick the dried leaves, be careful not to use any that have split or become moldy from being exposed to the elements too long.

PREPARATION Clean off any excess dirt and dry any moisture on the leaves.

STORAGE Bundle and store them in a cool, dry, airy, and dark place.

USE Soak the leaves in warm water for thirty to sixty minutes before using. (The soaking water may be used as a dye.) Split them in half and remove the stiff center part. They plait, twine, and coil very well. For coiling, they may be split and bundled for a foundation, and thin pieces may be used as the wrapping material.

Coiled Iris Leaves Basket by Dorothy Gill Barnes. 3½" tall, 4" in diameter. Photograph courtesy of the artist.

Kelp.

New Zealand flax.

Kelp

Kelp is a variety of brown seaweed found on ocean beaches. Its rope-like qualities and value range, from beige to brown, offer an interesting experience to the basket maker.

GATHERING Gather kelp at the beach when it is completely dry.

PREPARATION There is no preparation necessary, although you may soak it to remove the sand and then sort the pieces according to the color, value and size.

STORAGE Store it in a dry, cool, airy, dark place.

USE Kelp is soaked in hot water in the bath tub or in any other large vessel. This soaking makes it pliable and causes it to swell. Kelp is slippery so it is wise to experiment before commencing the actual basket construction. It works well for twining and looping.

Shape the basket by working it over a bowl or newspaper. It may be dried naturally or in a slow oven. Kelp will shrink as it dries and may twist out of shape. Twisting may be controlled by pushing the kelp back into place while drying. A kelp basket that *is not* pleasing may be soaked, taken apart, and reshaped.

New Zealand Flax

New Zealand Flax is an excellent basketry material because of its long leaves, strength, and variation of color. It is the material used by the Maori Indians of New Zealand for their rope-making and weaving. This plant grows in mild temperate zones; it thrives in Oregon and California.

GATHERING Cut the long leaves at any time.

PREPARATION The leaves may be left as is, or may be ripped in half where they fold. They also may be stripped into slender pieces and allowed to dry.

STORAGE If they are to be used fresh, store them in a bucket of fresh water (as you would keep flowers in a vase) until they are needed. If they are dried, they may be bundled and stored in a dry, cool, airy, dark place.

USE Flax becomes very stiff when dry. If you are working with dried material, soak it well. The dried shredded pieces may be used for coiling, either as the foundation or the wrapping material. Flat strips may be used for twining and plaiting. If the flax is being used fresh, keep in mind that it will shrink.

Dried and bundled lily of the Nile.

Kelp Basket II by author. 10″ in diameter, 4″ tall. Kelp has been worked in the twining technique in this basket.

Large willow tray by Judy Sohigian. 20″ diameter, 4″ tall. Willow branches form this wicker tray. Sisal rope is worked into the sides.

Large willow basket by Sylvia Seventy and Joe Schwinn. 20″ tall, 30″ long. This wicker basket is made of willow.

Lily of the Nile

This is an ornamental plant that grows in more temperate zones. The flower stalk of this lily offers a contrast to other material. After its preparation it is white and shiny.

GATHERING The stalks may be gathered when green after the spring flower dies, or may be gathered in the fall when they have dried. Pick stalks that are as long as possible and remove the dead flowers.

PREPARATION If the stalks are picked dry, they may be split, cleaned, and bundled for storage. If the stalks are gathered green, simmer them in hot water on the stove until the dark green color lightens. This will take about thirty minutes. The stalks may then be quartered lengthwise. Lay the quarters on a flat surface and scrape the pulp from them with a knife. Spread the scraped pieces on newspaper to dry. The pulp that is saved from this procedure may be used in papermaking.

STORAGE The dried pieces may be bundled and stored in a dry, cool, airy, dark place until they are needed.

USE Soak them in warm water for about thirty minutes. When they are pliable, they may be woven, plaited, or twined. They are very attractive when used as an accent with other wild materials.

Wild basket by Lucy Traber. 7' long, 20" wide. This long thin shape was looped with kelp of a light value on the inside, a dark value on the outside, and then framed with a large hollow piece of kelp on the perimeter. Photograph courtesy of the artist.

Wild basket by Lucy Traber. 18" in diameter, 26" tall. Palm and iron vine are twined to construct this basket. The surface interest is created by changing the direction of twist while twining. Notice the flat woven areas.

Wild basket by Lucy Traber. 18" tall, 5" in diameter. This basket has been twined of palm, using wide woven strips of fan palm bark for interest.

Wild basket by Lucy Traber. 23" long, 8" tall. This basket has been twined with a willow warp and a weft of palm, linen flax, agapanthus and cedar bark.

Wild basket by Lucy Traber. 9" in diameter, 8" tall. This basket was plaited and twined with New Zealand flax.

Wild basket by Lucy Traber. 26" long, 13" wide. Plaited in an under two, over two chevron pattern, this basket's sides were done in lattice twining. It is constructed exclusively of New Zealand flax.

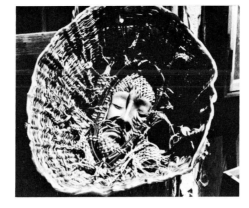

Burden Basket by Marcia Floor. 28" in length, 18" in diameter. Rawhide and leather strips have been woven over and under around branches of red osier (willow). Notice the brass ornament hanging on leather strips.

Basket by Carol Hart. 5½" by 5½". This wicker basket is made of boiled honeysuckle. Photograph courtesy of the artist.

Basket by Carol Hart. 10" wide, 5" tall. Lazy squaw stitch was used to create this basket of coiled iris leaves. Photograph courtesy of the artist.

Large Broom Grass and Reed Basket by Dorothy Gill Barnes. 12" tall, 34" in diameter. This basket of the wicker technique has a reed warp and broom grass for the weft. Photograph courtesy of the artist.

Wild Basket by Lucy Traber. 25" in diameter, 9" deep. This basket has been plaited on the bottom, and twined on the sides. Notice the direction change in the twining which gives movement to the sides. This basket is made of palm. Photograph courtesy of the artist.

Pine Needles

Pine trees grow in many parts of the world. Their long, thin needles range from pale green to a rich, dark brown, and when worked with raffia make very beautiful and economical baskets.

GATHERING Gather only long pine needles; the ideal length is from eight to ten inches. Pine needles may be gathered fresh from the tree. If a few are picked from various areas of the tree, the tree will be undamaged. They are best gathered in the summer after they have reached their full growth. You may also gather needles from under the pine tree. These needles will be various shades of brown because of exposure to the sun. Be sure to check them over for damage; if they have lain on the earth for a season or two, they may have rotten spots. If there are blemishes on the needles, discard them as they will break while you work.

PREPARATION If you pick the pine needles from the tree, dry them before using. To dry, lay them flat on a newspaper for about a month. It is important that they dry straight, as bent and curled needles are difficult to handle. If they curl while drying, soak them in hot water for about thirty minutes and bind them with rubber bands at the top and bottom to hold them straight.

If you dry your pine needles indoors, out of the sun, the color will remain green although it will lighten slightly.

After the needles dry, you may slip off the sheath that holds the needles together. Give the sheath a slight twist, and it will pull off easily. However, this sheath may also be left on to create interesting patterns.

STORAGE After the pine needles are dried and straightened they should be put in a brown paper bag and stored in a dry, cool, airy and dark place.

USE Soak the needles in water for about thirty minutes before beginning work. Soaking makes them pliable so they won't break. If you use hot water, they will soften sooner. While you are working on a basket, place the soaked needles between two

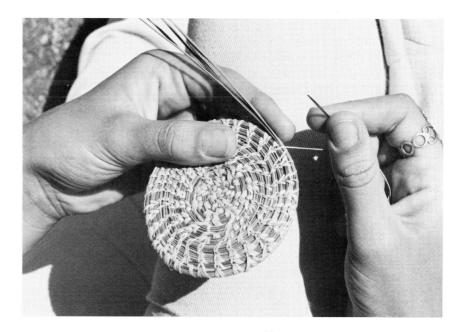

Hands working pine needles.

Pine needles drying on newspaper.

Side of basket showing pattern that may be created by leaving the sheath on the pine needles while working them.

damp towels or in a plastic bag to keep them moist. Don't leave them in the bag longer than one day as they may rot. After your basket gets about one inch in diameter, your needles do not need to be damp anymore.

When you make a pine needle basket, the pine needles are used as the foundation. Materials, such as raffia, yarn, cord, or long, thin strands of New Zealand flax are used as the wrapping material. Since raffia, a fiber that comes from the raffia palm tree in Madagascar, is the easiest material to use as the sewing or wrapping thread, let us briefly describe how to prepare and use it.

Soak raffia with the pine needles for about ten minutes. Then, depending upon its width, split it lengthwise into two or three pieces. Like many other sewing threads, raffia sometimes splits and wears as it is being worked. To prevent such splits, thread the darker, thicker end of the raffia through the eye of a sharp point crewel needle (a number 20). This way there won't be any pulling against the surface of the raffia while sewing. In addition, always keep the raffia damp while working.

Coiling Techniques for Pine Needle Basketry

The pine needle stitches are coiling techniques and do not have to be limited to the use of pine needles as the foundation material. One may experiment with foundations made of bundles of materials such as vines, grasses, straw, and corn shucks.

Since many of the pine needle techniques and stitches have been too often ignored by contemporary basket makers, they will be explored individually.

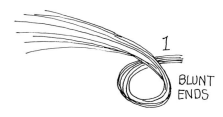

START There are many ways to start a pine needle basket. One way of starting is to take eight to ten needles, depending on their size, and form a loop about the size of a nickel. Make this loop at the blunt ends of the needles.

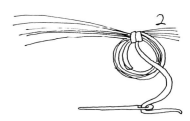

Wrap threaded raffia two or three times around the spot where the needles cross. It is important to wrap in the direction indicated in the illustrations: Forward through the inside of the loop, up over and around to the back, again bringing it forward through the loop. This is the direction in which the stitches will be sewn.

Start of a basket by Carole Lee.

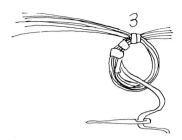

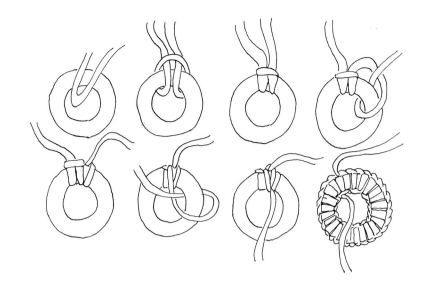

Continue to wrap around the loop about eight times until you reach the starting point, but don't completely cover the pine needles with raffia.

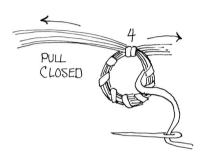

Now, pull the loop closed by pulling both ends of the pine needles.

WOVEN START Select a ring around which to work. A rubber washer or metal curtain ring will work well. Attach damp raffia to the ring as demonstrated in the illustrations. Making half hitches all around the ring, work one piece of the raffia on the inside of the ring, and one piece of the raffia on the outside, alternating from inside to outside, as indicated in the illustration. Work all the way around to completely cover the ring.

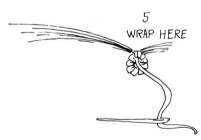

Again, wrap over the spot where the needles crossed. This act will secure the start. The idea is to have a tight circle with no opening. Practice two or three times to get a nice start. When completed, cut off the short, blunt ends of the needles on the right side. You have completed one row. It is important to keep track of your completed rows as you work around. Then, when you change stitches, you will know where to begin and where to end.

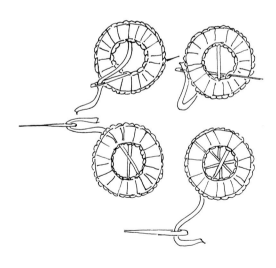

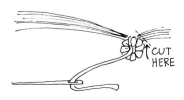

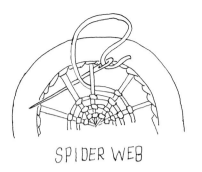

SPIDER WEB

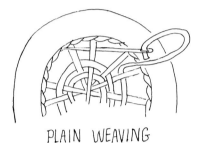

PLAIN WEAVING

When the ring is completely covered with raffia, make a lacey-looking piece of weaving on the inside of the ring. Thread the raffia into a sharp needle and make a warp by *sewing* it back and forth, going in and out of the half hitch knots on the inside of the ring. You may space these warps evenly, or not. If you want it to be even, count half hitch knots as you sew around.

When the sewing is finished, begin the weaving. This may be done several ways, in an even or an uneven pattern. A spider web design may be made by working the needle back, over one, and under two, back, over one, and under two, repeat. You may do a plain weave by going over, under, over, under, repeat. This method allows you to use your imagination to create an interesting design. When finished, conceal the end of the raffia in the half stitches.

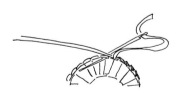

When the inside weaving is finished, you may begin adding pine needles to the outside of the ring. Do this by sticking the point of a pine needle (one needle at a time), under an existing half hitch knot. Sew it in place by making a plain stitch around the pine needle and through the half hitch knot. This stitch may be done

with raffia left over from covering the ring or with a new piece of raffia. Make two plain stitches in two successive half hitch knots to secure each pine needle, then add on another needle. Repeat this process. When you get completely around the ring once, you should have a full bundle of pine needles (about 10 needles). Now that the bundle is large and easier to handle, the needles may be added blunt end first, rather than pointed end first.

Whether using the plain start or the woven start as the beginning, you now proceed in the same manner. The start, your first row, is wrapped solidly with raffia. Consider each individual wrapping, with raffia, as one stitch. When practicing the following stitches, make at least three or four complete rows before trying a new stitch. This way you will be able to see the stitch as it progresses. A row of new stitches may be easily worked onto a row of another stitch. Also notice the direction in which the needle is stitching. This is the most comfortable way to work. If you change the wrapping direction, the angle in which the stitches are slanted will also change.

PLAIN STITCH To do this stitch, bring the sewing needle and raffia forward, up, over, and around the bundle of pine needles to the back where it passes through the top of a stitch from the previous row. Pick up each stitch and keep the stitches evenly spaced as you work around. You may pass the needle through part of the bundle of pine needles if you wish.

SPLIT STITCH This stitch is made by splitting the stitch of the previous row. Put the needle through the middle of the stitch, while also passing it through the middle of the bundle of pine needles.

DOUBLE SPLIT STITCH This stitch is made by making two stitches in the same place. First make the split stitch as you did before, but then instead of going on to the next stitch, put the needle through that same stitch again. Now, advance to the next stitch, and continue this process.

WHEAT STITCH Put the needle through the bundle of pine needles—not through the stitch—between two stitches of the previous row. Do this twice for each wheat stitch.

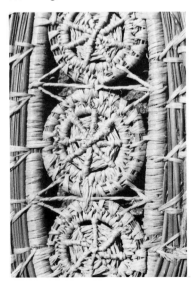

Woven starts worked in spider web design on pine needle tray. Courtesy of Anita and Jerry Rumburg.

WING STITCH This stitch makes a very pretty finish for the last row of a basket. It can also be used within the basket itself. Complete a row of the double split stitch. You have been working from right to left. Now, working from left to right, go back over this row of double split stitches by bringing the needle back and through the stitch previously split. You are making wing stitches. Cover the complete row of double split stitches with wing stitches. To do the next row, make another row of double split stitches; work from right to left. Cover them with wing stitches; work from left to right. Repeat these steps.

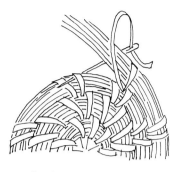

WHEAT STITCH

PLAIN STITCH

WING STITCH

SPLIT STITCH

Plain stitch on bread dough basket from Yugoslavia. Courtesy of Basket Bazaar, Yountville, California.

DOUBLE SPLIT STITCH

1.

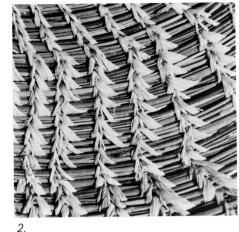

2.

3.

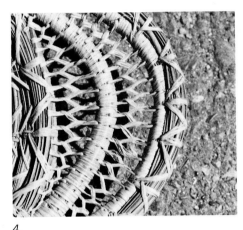

4.

1. Split stitch on bullrush bowl by the author.

2. Double split stitch on tray by the author.

3. Wheat stitch on pine needle basket by Carole Lee.

4. Wing stitch on the perimeter and in the body of the pine needle tray. Courtesy of Anita and Jerry Rumburg.

Pine needle tray. 12″ long, 7″ wide. Made about 1920. This basket has been worked with raffia over pine needles in the wheat stitch and the wing stitch. Courtesy of Anita and Jerry Rumburg.

New rows on tray by author.

New Rows

After you work a few rows of any of these stitches you will notice that the larger your piece becomes, the farther apart the rows of stitching become. It is necessary to add new rows so that your basket does not become loose and wobbly. Begin new rows by simply making a stitch between existing rows. When you add new rows, add them evenly all the way around. This evenness will keep your work looking neat.

A row of solid wrapping, and fragrant myrrh stitched in place finish bullrush bowl by author.

Wing stitch finishes pine needle tray. Courtesy of Anita and Jerry Rumburg.

Basket made with plain stitch shows tapered ending.

Adding Needles

When you feel the bundle of pine needles getting smaller, it is time to add another needle. Add needles, one at a time by inserting them blunt end first into the middle of the bundle. Keeping the bundle the same size will make your work appear neat. Also, try to keep the pine needles lying straight, instead of twisting around each other. This act will also make your work appear uniform.

Ending and Adding Raffia

There are two ways of adding new raffia. One way is to first hide the short end of the old raffia between the coiled rows. To do this, run the needle and raffia back between the row on which you are working, and the previous row. Start the new piece of raffia by hiding its end in the same place.

Another way is to pass the needle back and forth through the bundle of pine needles, making small hidden stitches near the place you are ending. Cut off the end of the raffia. Begin a new piece of raffia in the same way you ended, by making small hidden stitches near the point where the new stitch will begin. Proceed with the next stitch, keeping the same spacing.

Ending the Basket

Use your imagination in finishing the basket. As already mentioned, the wing stitch makes a pretty and finished looking last row. An attractive finish can be made by covering the last row completely with raffia. Also, you might finish with the stitch you have been using in the body of the basket. Whatever choice you make for the last row, finish off by tapering the needles down to a point. Refer back to the coiling chapter if you are unclear about this process.

After you finish your basket, you may want to shellac it. Shellac will add a very nice sheen to the basket and will help to preserve it. For best results, mix equal parts of shellac and wood alcohol, then brush on. Two to four coats should cover your basket well.

Small pine needle basket by Lee DeKoker. 3" by 3". Made with the wheat stitch. Courtesy of Lydia Van Gelder.

Pine needle basket by Carole Lee.

Small pine needle basket by author. 2½" diameter, 1" tall. Made with the split stitch.

Basket with lid, basket maker unknown. 9" in diameter, 5" tall. The pine needles were coiled leaving the sheaths in place. Cotton cord is the wrapping material worked in the plain stitch. After completion, the basket was varnished.

Basket by Shereen LaPlantz. 12" tall, 6" wide, 4" deep. The body of this basket was loom woven with a linen warp and split cane weft, then was nailed to a wooden base. Photograph by David M. LaPlantz.

NON TRADI- TIONAL BASKET TECH- NIQUES

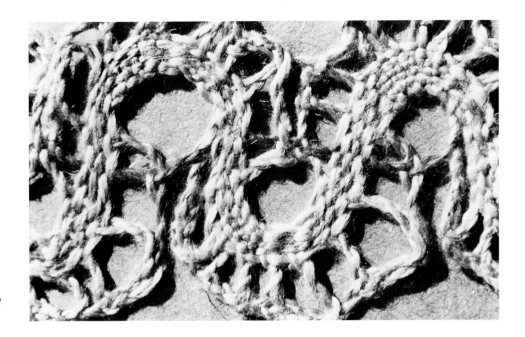

Closeup of a lace sample piece by the author.

Closeup of a crocheted sample piece by the author.

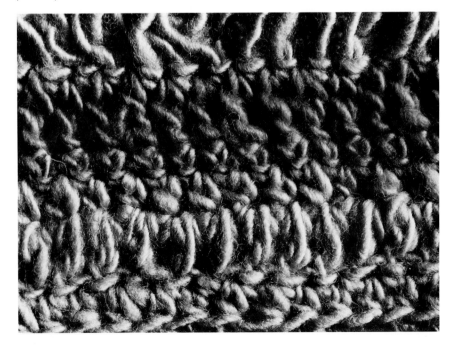

Basket making need not be limited to traditional basket techniques. Many fiber construction techniques may be formed into basket shapes. Experiment first with techniques with which you are familiar, then try those techniques which are new to you. Listed below are a few possibilities for further study.

Bobbin Lace

This type of lace is made from the interlacing of vertical warp threads and is chiefly used for flat pieces. Numerous patterns may be used in various combinations. The direction and tension of elements may be altered to form basket shapes.

Crochet

Crochet is a single element lace technique that builds up in rows. It easily gives the appearance of the coiling technique if worked in a circular manner. By using a variety of crochet stitches and by altering the tension control, you can make appealing baskets.

Felt

Felt is a material made of matted wool fibers and is created by moisture, temperature change, and friction. It may be used to create basket shapes by shaping the wool before it is felted, or by cutting shapes from the wool after it is felted.

Knotting or Macramé

Knotting is a lace technique made from knotting vertical threads together. Horizontal and diagonal threads may also be knotted. The half hitch may be worked in a circular direction to closely resemble the coiling technique.

Closeup of a felt sample piece by the author.

Closeup from a knotted handbag by the author.

Closeup from a looped basket of kelp by the author.

Closeup from a piece of recycled paper by the author.

Looping or Knotless Netting

Looping is a single element construction technique made from a long continuous fiber. Looping has netlike or stretch qualities. It may be used to form basket shapes if the material used has body to it.

Papermaking

Paper is usually thought of as a flat fibrous material made from rags, wood, and recycled paper. However, it may be molded into three-dimensional basketry shapes.

Closeup of stitching from *Panty-hose Basket* by Peggy Moulton.

Stitchery

A contemporary type of embroidery, stitchery may be used to mold pieces of fabric together into basket shapes. Various stitches and fabrics used with appliqué combine to make this an exciting technique for basketry.

Alice Basket by author. 8" tall, 4" in diameter. Natural dyed wool and yarn were felted to form the basket. The stitching and the faces were added after completion.

Bobbin Lace Basket by Lydia Van Gelder. 4" tall, 4" in diameter. Beige, gold jute, and linen cord are worked in the bobbin lace technique to form this basket.

Tie Basket by Marcia Floor. 36″ in diameter, 36″ tall. Made from men's neckties, this basket is made with half hitches and rests over a metal framework.

Rayon Basket by Gary Trentham. 20″ in diameter, 12″ tall. This basket is made by coiling and knots. The ends of yarn are twisted until they bunch up. Photograph by John Creel.

Cotton Rope Basket by Gary Trentham. 38″ in diameter, 11″ tall. This basket is constructed of cotton, string, and rope. The inner part of the basket has been coiled and the outer part half hitched. Photograph by John Creel.

Raffia Basket by Gary Trentham. 9″ tall, 17″ in diameter. This basket is constructed of raffia with erratic half hitches. Photograph by David Arky.

Woven Box by Dorothy Gill Barnes. 8" by 8" by 7" tall. This piece was woven on a loom with waxed linen as the warp and sweet grass as the weft. Blue grass extends at the corners. Photograph courtesy of the artist.

Egg Basket by Diane Itter. 3¼" tall, 3" in diameter. The direction of the half hitches changes constantly around this basket. It was finished by allowing the ends of linen to cover the inside. Photograph courtesy of the artist.

Felt Basket by Lisa Wagner. 9" tall, 12" in diameter. This white felt basket was made by coiling wool rolag into a basket shape with handspun wool yarn. Then it was felted together with carded fleece on the outside of the basket.

Coral Basket by Ellen Jones. 12" by 15". This basket has been knotted of jute and linen. Photograph by Arthur Jones.

Basket by Lida Gordon. 14″ tall, 12″ in diameter. Made of natural silks, this soft basket has been hand stitched and stuffed. Photograph courtesy of the artist.

Basket by Larry Edman. This basket is made of silk wrapping material on a linen foundation and has been half hitched from a coiled base. The lid is also coiled. Photograph courtesy of the artist.

Paper baskets by Lisa Wagner. 9" tall, 12" in diameter. Cotton rag paper pulp has been pressed into a latex mold to form these two baskets.

Bibliography

Allen, Elsie. *Pomo Basketmaking*. Healdsburg, California: Naturegraph Publishers, 1972.

Grae, Ida. *Nature's Colors, Dyes from Plants*. New York: Macmillan Publishing Co., Inc., 1974.

Hammel, William C. A. *Pine-Needle Basketry in Schools*. Seattle, Washington: Shorey Publications, 1972.

Hart, Carol and Dan. *Natural Basketry*. New York: Watson Guptill Publications, 1976.

Harvey, Virginia I. *The Techniques of Basketry*. New York: Van Nostrand Reinhold Co., 1974.

James, George Wharton. *Indian Basketry*. New York: Dover Publications, Inc., 1972.

Meilach, Dona Z. *A Modern Approach to Basketry*. New York: Crown Publishers, 1974.

Merrill, Ruth Earl. *Plants Used In Basketry by the California Indians*. Ramona, California: Ballena Press, 1973.

Navajo School of Indian Basketry, *Indian Basket Weaving*. New York: Dover Publications, Inc., 1971.

Newman, Sandra Corrie. *Indian Basket Weaving*. Flagstaff, Arizona: Northland Press, 1974.

Paque, Joan Michaels. *Design Principles and Fiber Techniques*. Shorewood, Wisconsin, 1973.

Rainey, Sarita R. *Weaving Without A Loom*. Worcester, Massachusetts: Davis Publications, Inc., 1966.

Tod, Osma Gallinger. *Earth Basketry*. New York: Bonanza Books, a division of Crown Publishers, Inc., 1972.